Collins

CAPE® REVISION GUIDE
COMMUNICATION STUDIES

T0312368

Natalee Cole
Brenda Lee Browne

HarperCollins Publishers Ltd
The News Building
1 London Bridge Street
London SE1 9GF

HarperCollins *Publishers*
Macken House,
39/40 Mayor Street Upper,
Dublin1,
D01C9W8,
Ireland

First edition 2017

10 9 8 7 6 5

© HarperCollins *Publishers* Limited 2017

ISBN 978-0-00-815729-6

Collins® is a registered trademark of HarperCollins Publishers Limited

CAPE® Revision Guide: Communication Studies is an independent publication and has not been authorised, sponsored or otherwise approved by CXC®.

CAPE® is a registered trademark of the **Caribbean Examinations Council (CXC®)**.

www.collins.co.uk/caribbean

A catalogue record for this book is available from the British Library.

Typeset by QBS Learning

Printed and bound in the UK by Ashford Colour Press Ltd

All rights reserved. No part of this book may be reproduced, stored in a retrieval system, or transmitted in any form or by any means, electronic, mechanical, photocopying, recording or otherwise, without the prior permission in writing of the Publisher. This book is sold subject to the conditions that it shall not, by way of trade or otherwise, be lent, resold, hired out or otherwise circulated without the Publisher's prior consent in any form of binding or cover other than that in which it is published and without a similar condition including this condition being imposed on the subsequent purchaser.

If any copyright holders have been omitted, please contact the Publisher who will make the necessary arrangements at the first opportunity.

Publisher: Elaine Higgleton
Commissioning Editor: Lucy Cooper
Development Editor: Penny Nicholson
Managing Editor: Sarah Thomas
Project Manager: Alissa McWhinnie
Copy Editor: Penny Nicholson
Proofreader: Helen Bleck
Answer Checker: Catherine Dakin
Proof Editor: Aidan Gill
Artwork: QBS Learning
Cover design: Kevin Robbins and Gordon MacGilp
Production: Lauren Crisp

This book is produced from independently certified FSC™ paper to ensure responsible forest management.

For more information visit: www.harpercollins.co.uk/green

Contents

Introduction

Purpose of the Revision Guide

The purpose of this Communication Studies Revision Guide is to support candidates as they prepare for the Caribbean Examinations Council CAPE® Communication Studies examination. It has been written by practising teachers of the examination.

It should be noted, however, that in order to gain full benefit from the content provided, particularly in relation to preparing a portfolio for the Internal Assessment (IA) component of the examination, students are advised to make full use of this guide from the outset of their studies and not exclusively in the final stages of preparation for the examination.

Approach of the Revision Guide

The Revision Guide adopts a two-pronged approach.

- There is a chapter supporting students with guidance on how to tackle each of the three components of the Caribbean Examinations Council CAPE® Communication Studies examination – Paper 1, Paper 2 and the Internal Assessment.
- There is a chapter covering the content and objectives of each of the syllabus modules. Each of these chapters is organised around the structure of the Caribbean Examinations Council CAPE® Communication Studies examination. This ensures complete syllabus coverage in terms of content and the stated syllabus objectives, which are outlined both at the beginning of each chapter and at the beginning of each section within the chapter.

  The Caribbean Examinations Council CAPE® Communication Studies examination requires students to not only know the content of the syllabus but also to employ higher-order comprehension skills to interpret, evaluate and apply that knowledge. The three chapters devoted to the module content not only help students revise this content, they also help them to understand the content at the higher level required for them to produce good-quality essays for Paper 2 and a superior portfolio.

The Revision Guide uses bulleted lists, tables and short paragraphs in order to provide the content in a condensed and accessible style.

Organisation of the Revision Guide

- Chapter 1 provides guidance and support for students in approaching Sections A and B of Paper 1 of the examination.

  As well as advice on tackling multiple-choice questions in general, there are specific tips to help with Section A, the listening comprehension. There are worked examples with teacher commentary throughout the chapter and the worked examples for Section A are supported by an audio recording available at collins.co.uk/caribbean. There are tips and a section on time management to further help students improve their performance on this paper.

- Chapters 2–4 cover the content and objectives of syllabus Module 1: Gathering and Processing Information, Module 2: Language and Community and Module 3: Speaking and Writing, respectively.

  There are exam tips and notes throughout and each chapter ends with exam-style multiple-choice questions for students to practise the techniques learnt in Chapter 1 and gauge their understanding of the module content.

  Chapter 2 provides two practice listening comprehensions which are supported by audio recordings.

- Chapter 5 provides guidance and support for students in approaching Paper 2 of the examination.

  It offers general advice on writing essays, including a section on linking structures and transitional devices, to help students maximise the marks they obtain for organisation and expression in their essays.

  In addition, it offers specific advice for writing the essay for each of the modules. The format of the questions is analysed and guidance is given to help students maximise the marks they obtain for content in their essays.

  There is an example of an essay for each of the modules and these are annotated to highlight how the essay puts the advice given into practice to answer the question.

  The chapter ends with a practice question for each of the three Paper 2 questions.

- Chapter 6 provides practical support for students in preparation for and production of the portfolio required for the Internal Assessment component of the examination. It gives help with choosing and researching a theme. It also gives students advice about the requirements of each section of the portfolio and how to maximise the marks they attain.

- At the end of the book, the audioscripts of the recordings for the listening comprehension in Chapter 1 and the two listening comprehensions in Chapter 2 are printed to allow further analysis or for use if students are unable to access the recordings from the website. There are also the answers to all the practice questions for Paper 1. Finally, there is an index to enable students to look up any particular subject they wish to revise.

Chapter 1

Techniques for Paper 1

Objectives

By the end of this chapter you should be able to do these things:

- recognise cue words in MCQs;
- use cue words in stimulus, question or options to assist in identifying the correct answer;
- effectively eliminate incorrect responses;
- practise active listening;
- identify items based on objectives specific to each module.

Exam Tip

Be sure to take a pencil to the exam.

Introduction

Paper 1 has only recently been made into a multiple-choice paper. The aim is to test your knowledge and understanding of the main concepts across the syllabus. For this paper you are presented with 45 items organised into two sections – A and B. The items test either comprehension or language awareness and use. The stimulus material may be in the form of words, illustrations or a combination of both. Paper 1 accounts for 30% of your final grade.

Section A is the listening comprehension. It focuses on your ability to actively listen and then respond to the items on the exam paper. You will need to fully concentrate in order to understand the piece being read to you. This section has seven items and is based on Module 1.

Section B comprises 38 items. Items 8–15 are based on Module 1, items 16–30 are based on Module 2 and items 31–45 are based on Module 3. It is imperative that you are familiar with the objectives of the syllabus. This will help you to do well on this paper.

The aim of this chapter is to assist you in perfecting the techniques needed to complete Paper 1.

Techniques for Section A

Section A is the listening comprehension.

You will be given two minutes to read through the items before the extract is read to you. Remember there are 7 test items, each with four options. You have about 15 seconds to read each item.

The extract will be from a poem or from a work of prose fiction.

The items in Section A will be based on:

- the main idea of the extract;
- details supporting the main idea;
- the purpose of the extract;
- strategies used to achieve the purpose;
- literary devices used in the extract;
- the type of discourse;
- the effectiveness of devices or techniques used in the extract;
- the meanings of expressions used in the extract.

Step 1: Read the questions and options

You already know the items that will be in this section – they are always the same kinds of items (see list above) with slight variations. It is important though for you to read each item nevertheless.

As you read the items and options, focus on the key words and expressions.

Underline the key words and expressions in the items.

Read the items and options aloud (in hushed tones) if that will help you to register what you need to listen for.

1. The <u>MAIN idea</u> of the extract is that Christmas

    A. is a time of celebration.

    B. brought a positive change and created a light-hearted, festive atmosphere.

    C. caused prices to drop and people to stop fighting.

    D. is the best time of the year.

> When you read this item you know you will be listening for the writer's key concept.
>
> The answer you select should reflect the gist of what the extract is saying.
>
> You already know that this extract will have something to do with Christmas. Now you need to listen for the details that tell you 'what about Christmas'.
>
> The options should give you a clue about what you should listen for.
>
> The options tend to capture bits and pieces of information from the piece but remember the function of the distractors – they may look like a possible answer because they carry a word or two mentioned in the extract, but ask yourself 'Is that what the extract is really about?'.

3. The <u>expression 'Never were destitutes more deserving'</u> suggests that

    A. at Christmas poor people deserve help.

    B. Christmas brought more destitutes.

    C. at Christmas, more than any other time, people feel justified in giving to the poor.

    D. destitutes did well throughout the year and should be rewarded at Christmas.

> This item is asking you to interpret the expression based on the context of the extract.
>
> While you are reading through the options, eliminate responses that you know right away are unsuitable.
>
> Use what you have learnt in other test items.
>
> Item 1 tells you that the extract is about Christmas, so this item therefore has to do with the Christmas season. The fact that this item is based at the interpretive level of comprehension should be a clue to tell you that the response you choose cannot express a literal idea.

worthy of / justified

Indirect comparison; choked – human – like; strident – loud, grating

4. What is the <u>literary device</u> used in 'The streets <u>choked with slow but strident traffic'</u>?

    A. ~~Synecdoche~~

    B. Metaphor

    C. Personification

    D. ~~Paradox~~

> For the items on literary devices you may not need to wait for the passage to select a response.
>
> You can cross out and/or tick the options as you read them based on how the item is phrased.

> Note that you can eliminate options (A) and (D). Neither of those are devices of comparison. You need to use the meanings of the other two devices to decide between them.
>
> You could also use the meanings of the devices to select the correct option straightaway.

Note: You **must know** the different literary devices.

Some items may give you a list of literary devices and you have to determine which are used in the extract. In that case, you must quickly remind yourself what each device is and as the reader reads the extract you listen for the devices and jot them down as you hear them.

Step 2: Listen for the gist of the extract

The first time the passage is read, do not attempt to make any notes.

Focus fully on the words and sentences of the extract.

Your aim is to understand the main idea of the text.

When the speaker pauses, try to quickly and succinctly jot down in note form what the extract is about.

Listen to the extract now. It is available at https://www.collins.co.uk/page/Caribbean. (Alternatively, you can read it on page 154.)

> The notes you write here should assist you with responding to all seven test items, so you need to listen carefully so that you can get as much information as you possibly can.
>
> Item 2 generally asks about details relating to the main idea so these notes should help you to answer that item.
>
> Remember though that you are not allowed to start answering the items until the examiner gives you the go-ahead.

Example of notes made during pause

Bad year, things scarce

Christmas, crowded, people shopping, streets choked = traffic jam

Clumsy toys, bright signs, decorations

Gaiety (cheerfulness)

Year ending well

Step 3: Listening for specific information and detailed understanding

When the extract is being read the second time, keep in mind the seven items you will need to respond to.

You will be listening for specific details based on the key words you underlined in each test item.

As you pick up key words and details make your jottings, preferably next to the test item to which they are relevant.

Do not be dismayed if you are not able to write notes for each item.

Instructions: You will hear an extract. It will be read twice. Listen carefully before answering the items based on the extract.

1. The MAIN idea of the extract is that Christmas
   A. is a time of celebration.
   B. brought a positive change and created a light-hearted, festive atmosphere.
   C. caused prices to drop and people to stop fighting.
   D. is the best time of the year.

   > People shopping, decorations everywhere (bright sign, Santa Claus, reindeer, snow)
   > People seem happy

2. Which of the following details support the main idea?
   I.   Rosy-cheeked Santa Clauses
   II. Fights in shops
   III. Prancing reindeer
   A. I and II only
   B. I and III only
   C. II and III only
   D. I, II and III

3. The expression 'Never were destitutes more deserving' suggests that
   A. at Christmas poor people deserve help.
   B. Christmas brought more destitutes.
   C. at Christmas, more than any other time, people feel justified in giving to the poor.
   D. destitutes did well throughout the year and should be rewarded at Christmas.

4. What is the literary device used in 'The streets choked with slow but strident traffic'.
   A. ~~Synecdoche~~
   B. Metaphor
   C. Personification
   D. ~~Paradox~~

   > Indirect comparison; choked – human-like; strident – loud, grating

5. What is the main literary device used in the extract?
   A. Personification //
   B. Imagery ////
   C. Metaphor
   D. Irony

   > For an item like this, you may not be able to make note of all the examples and, in fact, you don't need to.
   >
   > Instead make a mark next to the relevant option each time you hear an example of that literary device.

6. Which of the following types of discourse is used by the writer in this extract?

   A. Narration

   B. Exposition

   C. Argumentation

   D. Description

> These are the kind of notes you would make for this item as you read through the items.
>
> As you hear the passage read you can put a tick or a cross beside the definitions.

Tell a story ×

Give info ×

Argue points / persuade ×

Paint pic / describe scene √

7. Which of the following comments BEST expresses the effectiveness of the phrase 'the urgent gaiety that belonged to the season'?

   A. It presents a visual picture of the flurry and excitement that came with Christmas.

   B. It creates a sense of urgency in the audience.

   C. It shows that Christmas has a sense of happiness.

   D. It helps the audience to visualise how happy the people were.

> Remember when you are asked about effectiveness, you are really being asked 'How well did something work?'. Therefore, think about what the expression does, what it helps you to understand, feel, think and imagine about what is presented to you in the extract.

Step 4: Once you are told to begin, do so.

The first three have been done for you. Review the test items and notes above.
     Maybe listen to the extract again, and practise with items 4–7.
     Check your answers online at https://www.collins.co.uk/page/Caribbean or on page 156.

1. (A) **(B)** (C) (D)

2. (A) **(B)** (C) (D)

3. (A) (B) **(C)** (D)

4. (A) (B) (C) (D)

5. (A) (B) (C) (D)

6. (A) (B) (C) (D)

7. (A) (B) (C) (D)

General pointers

Before listening

- Prepare to listen. Focus on key words and expressions in the items. and options.

While listening

- Focus on key words and expressions. (Remember you underlined them in the items before you.)
- Take notes to support your memory.
- Focus on the intonation of the reader. (This usually helps with understanding the extract.)

After listening

- Think about the extract again. Ask yourself if you have understood the main points.
- Repeat to yourself (mentally) what the extract is about.
- Summarise what you understand the main idea to be.
- Before going on to respond to the test items review your notes.

Study Tip

To practise listening comprehension skills, select some poems from your CXC® Poetry text and get in groups with your friends and go through as many as you can.

Each of you take a turn reading a poem and then attempt to write responses based on the different areas you know this section will cover.

Share and discuss your responses with each other.

There are also two listening comprehensions for you to practise with at the end of Chapter 2.

Techniques for Section B

Section B has 38 multiple-choice items. There are eight items based on Module 1, 15 based on Module 2 and 15 on Module 3.

Most of the test items will be based on stimuli composed of words or a combination of words and pictures.

Each test item will have four options – one correct response and three distractors.

In general, two of the distractors will be definitely incorrect but the third may look very close to the correct response.

Step 1: Read the questions and options

Before you read the relevant stimulus, read the test items that relate to it.

Each stimulus will have between three and five related test items.

The aim is to understand what the test item is asking and to familiarise yourself with the responses. This will make it easier to identify the correct response.

As you read the items, focus on the key words and expressions.

Underline the key words and expressions in the items.

Exam Tip

Try hiding the options for each test item until after you have read the stem.

This way you can work out in your head if you know the answer.

Then read the options to see if one matches the answer you came up with.

---

8. Which combination gives two data collection methods that would be most suitable for Chrisanna?
    A. Observation and surveys
    B. Interviews and observations
    C. Questionnaires and observations
    D. Interviews and surveys

Ask yourself 'What is the question asking?'

It requires you to select a response that has two data collection methods **and** they must be the **most suitable** of all the choices.

'Most suitable' suggests that more than one option has potential but one is a better choice.

---

9. From which of the following sources would Chrisanna get valuable and irrefutable data?
    I.   The students
    II.   The teachers
    III. Social media platforms
    A. I and II only
    B. I and III only
    C. II and III only
    D. I, II and III

This item is asking you to identify the sources which would not only provide Chrisanna with data that would be helpful but data that is unquestionable. The latter element indicates that the data must therefore be taken directly from the source.

The options provide you with three sources, either two or three of them will be suitable sources. Therefore, when you read the stimulus, you will need to identify the sources indicated in the scenario. This will help you to select the correct response.

---

10. Chrisanna plans to make generalisations in her article. In order for it to be acceptable for her to do this she would need to:
    A. collect data from all 1870 students.
    B. use only ¼ of the student population and some from other schools.
    C. use a representative sample.
    D. support her data with evidence from research.

To answer this item you need to know what it means to make generalisation and you also need to remember what you have been taught about when not to make generalisations and what factors would make generalisations acceptable.

Step 2: Read the stimulus

After you have read the related test items and gained an understanding of what each test item requires, read the stimulus once to get a gist of what it is saying

Then read the stimulus a second time, this time underlining any key words or expressions that will assist in responding to the test items, based on the key words and expressions you underlined in the questions.

Instructions: Read the following scenario carefully and then answer Items 8–10.

Chrisanna is a senior reporter for her school newspaper and has been asked to write an article on which type of social media gets more of her schoolmates' attention – Instagram, Snapchat or Twitter and how often it is used. She has decided to conduct some research to inform her writing.

Step 3: Eliminate the incorrect distractors

If after reading the test items, options and stimulus, you have not identified the correct response, you can apply the process of elimination.

Remember that it is likely that two of the four will definitely be incorrect and one will look like the correct response. What you need to do now is identify the two obviously incorrect options.

8. Which combination gives two data collection methods that would be most suitable for Chrisanna?
   A. Observation and surveys
   B. Interviews and observations
   C. Questionnaires and observations
   D. Interviews and surveys

The question is asking you to identify two data collection methods. First go through the options and determine whether or not they are actually data collection methods.

A survey is a type of research design and not a data collection method so you can eliminate all the options that contain survey – options (A) and (D).

You are now left with options (B) and (C). Both options comprise two data collection methods so you must eliminate the third distractor based on suitability – the other requirement of the test item – most suitable.

Both options (B) and (C) contain observations as part of the combination so the choice is really between interviews and questionnaires.

Go back to your stimulus. What is Chrisanna doing? She is conducting research involving her schoolmates. This is likely to be a relatively large number of people.

Think back on the advantages of using questionnaires and interviews as methods for collecting data.

Which is more suitable for collecting data from a large population?

Knowing that it is the questionnaire, you can eliminate option (B) and so the correct answer is option (C).

9. From which of the following sources would Chrisanna get valuable and irrefutable data?
   I. The students
   II. The teachers
   III. Social media platforms
   A. I and II only
   B. I and III only
   C. II and III only
   D. I, II and III

Remember that the option selected should not only provide data that is helpful but data that cannot be challenged as it comes from a primary source.

According to the stimulus, Chrisanna is collecting data about her schoolmates' use of social media. That therefore eliminates teachers because although the information from this source may be helpful it would not be 'irrefutable'.

Put a cross beside this source and tick the other two sources to remind yourself what you have decided.

You can then eliminate any options which include teachers – options (A), (C) and (D).

You are left with option (B) as the correct response.

10. Chrisanna plans to <u>make generalisations</u> in her article. In order for it to be <u>acceptable for her to do this</u> she would need to:

A. ~~collect data from all 1870 students.~~

B. ~~use only ¼ of the student population and some from other schools.~~

C. use a representative sample.

D. ~~support her data with evidence from research.~~

Start with option (A). Does Chrisanna need to collect data from **all** members of the student body in order to make generalisations? No, so you can eliminate option (A).

Option (B) suggests using only ¼ of the student population and some from other schools.

Why ¼? What criteria will be used to select which students to use? Does she need data from other schools?

It looks like a possible response but smells like a distractor. Leave it for now.

Option (C) says use a representative sample.

You should know that a representative sample is one that gives a true reflection of the population and can therefore be used to make generalisations. (It would be unacceptable to make generalisations based on a sample that was not representative.)

You can see that option (C) is the correct response so by default you can eliminate options (B) and (D).

Worked examples

Note: In the exam the stimulus will always precede the question but in order to practise applying the techniques the questions are presented first.

Step 1

Read the items and options and underline the key terms and expressions in the items.

> **Exam Tip**
>
> If you can recognise the answer immediately, as here, you may not need to use the process of elimination.

> **Exam Tip**
>
> Remember that the MCQs may test comprehension or language awareness and use, or both.
>
> Bear this in mind as you read the questions and try to determine what is being tested.
>
> This can be helpful.

1. <u>Why would the mother think</u> that her daughter 'kyaahn get ahead wid dat'?

A. Creole is not the official language.

B. ~~Creole is not a language.~~

C. ~~Creole lacks mutual intelligibility.~~

D. Creole doesn't enhance social status.

This item requires you to make an inference based on the use of an expression (comprehension) but it also tests your awareness of language and its use.

You need to know the definition and features of a Creole language, for instance.

When you read the stimulus, you know to pay attention to the expression 'kyaahn get ahead wid dat' and try to understand why the mother said it.

Note that for this question, you can eliminate the two clearly incorrect options immediately, without needing to read the stimulus.

You should already know that Creole is mutually intelligible and that it is a language and so options (B) and (C) are quite clearly, in this case, two of the three distractors.

2. Which combination of emotions shows <u>Shantol's and her mother's contrasting attitudes</u> to Creole?

A. Admiration and disgust

B. Pride and shame

C. Shame and admiration

D. Pride and disapproval

This item is mostly comprehension-based but it does also require you to understand how attitudes to language are conveyed.

Note that you are looking for two attitudes that differ, specifically for Shantol and her mother. Also note that in the test item Shantol is named first, then her mother. This means that in the option you choose her attitude should be reflected first.

This question also depends on your vocabulary – knowing what each word in the options mean.

3. According to the mother, what role should education play in her daughter's use of language?

   A. ~~Education should help her to succeed in life.~~

   B. ~~Education should teach her to be better than her mother.~~

   C. Education should teach her how to speak English well.

   D. Education should help her daughter to stop speaking Creole.

> This item is testing comprehension (possibly at the literal level) so note the key terms.
>
> You need to focus on the options because when you are reading the stimulus you need to determine which of these options are suggested by the mother either directly or indirectly.

> You could eliminate any of the distractors that you can securely say are wrong at this point.
>
> Option (A) says that education should help the daughter to succeed in life. However, the test item is asking about how education affects the daughter's use of language. Option (A) does not reflect that. Neither does option (B), so you can safely say that these two options are distractors, even before you read the stimulus.

Exam Tip

It is always good to look for clues in both the phrasing of the test items and the options themselves.

4. What feature of Caribbean English Creole grammar is exemplified in the expression 'Teacher mad!'?

   A. Subject–verb agreement

   B. Zero-copula construction

   C. Absence of tense marker

   D. Front-focusing

> This item is testing language awareness and use.
>
> To answer this item you need to know features of English Creole.
>
> This item is asking you to identify a feature that is specific to the grammar of English Creole.
>
> For such an item, you do not need the stimulus. The test item contains all the information you need so now all you would need to do is match that with the various options and select the correct one.
>
> If you do not know or if you are unsure, use the process of elimination when you are ready to start responding to the test items.
>
> It is important that you familiarise yourself with the linguistic features of English Creole.
>
> When you look at the options can you say what each of them is?
>
> It is likely that you are familiar with subject–verb agreement and tense marking but what about zero-copula construction and front-focusing?

5. Which of the following does NOT reflect the phonology of Caribbean English Creole?

   A. 'Is a homework'

   B. ~~'Shet yu mout'~~

   C. ~~'get ahead wid dat'~~

   D. ~~'mi a go call yu mada'~~

> This item also tests language awareness and use.
>
> The preceding item asked about grammar; this item asks about phonology.
>
> To answer this item correctly you need to know that phonology has to do with the sound system or pronunciation of English Creole. You will also need to be aware of the differences between Caribbean Standard English pronunciation and Creole pronunciation.
>
> Again, you do not need the stimulus. The test item contains all the information you need. (This does not mean that you do not need to read the stimulus carefully.)
>
> Also pay attention to the key words. Note that the test item says 'does NOT'.

> Since you are looking for the one that does **not** sound Creole, simply read the options aloud (quietly though, you are, after all, in an examination) and eliminate any of the options that contains even one word with a Creole pronunciation.
>
> This eliminates all the options except option (A) and so that is your choice.
>
> Note that option (A) may not sound as though it is Standard English, and indeed it isn't – it is reflective of Creole grammar but in this question the focus is phonology.

Step 2

Read the stimulus.

Keep in mind the key terms and expressions you underlined in the questions and underline the key terms and expressions in the stimulus that will help you answer the items.

Instructions: Read the following scenario carefully and then answer Items 1–5.

Best friends Shantol and Amira are translating a poem written in Standard English into Creole when Shantol's mother, who is passing by the bedroom, overhears.

Mother: Is patwa yu inside here wid gyal?

Shantol: No Mommy.

Mother: Den wah dat mi ear yu se to Amira?

Amira: Is a homework wi doing Miss Vie. Teacher say wi must translate the poem to patwa.

Mother: Teacher mad! Mi a send you to school so you can come out beta dan mi gyal. Where patwa can kyari yu. Yu don't do not'n more pon dat homework. I going down tu di school tomorrow tomorrow mawnin. Teacher know ow aad mi a fi struggle, shi a blighted yu future … bout translate English in a patwa!!

Shantol: But Mommy patwa is a language. It have its own function and …

Mother: Shet yu mout gyal. You doan know what good fi yu, bout language! Patwa is gibberish. Yu kyaahn get ahead wid dat so you try talk proper. A dat mi send you to school fa. As fi you Miss Amira, as I done tidy up the place mi a go call yu mada.

> When you read the stimulus, because you have already read the test items you know what details you are reading for so underline relevant details. You could also make notes in the margin.
>
> For instance, one test item asked about Shantol's and her mother's attitudes to language, so when you read their speech make a note of how they seem to feel about the language based on what they say. Punctuation can help you in this too.

Step 3

Go back to the test items, re-read them and select your response.

Remember: if you do not know the answer or if you are unsure, use the process of elimination.

1. Why would the mother think that her daughter 'kyaahn get ahead wid dat'?
    A. Creole is not the official language.
    B. Creole is not a language.
    C. Creole lacks mutual intelligibility.
    D. Creole doesn't enhance social status.

> Remember when you were reading through the test items you eliminated options (B) and (C) based on your knowledge of language. So the two contenders here now are options (A) and (D).
>
> Option (A) says Creole is not the official language. That is true but is that the mother's contention in the scenario you were presented with? No. At no point in the dialogue did she mention the status of the language, but she did say things like – 'Where patwa can kyari yu', 'shi a blighted yu future', in addition to the expression included in the test item. All of this speaks to social mobility and based on what you know of the Creole language and its status in society you know it does not help with moving up in society – higher education, getting jobs and promotions etc. So the correct option is (D).

2. Which combination of emotions shows Shantol's and her mother's contrasting attitudes to Creole?
    A. Admiration and disgust
    B. Pride and shame
    C. Shame and admiration
    D. Pride and disapproval

> Option (A) can be eliminated because disgust is the wrong emotion for the mother. She did not appear to be disgusted by either language.
>
> Neither is she ashamed. We know she regards Standard English highly and she uses English Creole herself so shame does not reflect her feelings, nor does it reflect the feeling of the daughter so options (B) and (C) are effectively eliminated.
>
> The remaining option and therefore the correct response is (D). The mother disapproves of her daughter using Creole and of the teacher giving a Creole-based assignment; while Shantol seems proud, claiming that Creole is a language with its own functions.

3. According to the mother, what role should education play in her daughter's use of language?

   A. ~~Education should help her to succeed in life.~~

   B. ~~Education should teach her to be better than her mother.~~

   C. Education should teach her how to speak English well.

   D. ~~Education should help her daughter to stop speaking Creole.~~

> When you read the test items, you used the requirements of the test item to eliminate options (A) and (B) so now you are considering (C) and (D).
>
> The information you require to distinguish between them is in the stimulus.
>
> If necessary, go back to the stimulus and look for where the mother makes reference to either option (C) or (D).
>
> She says 'you try talk proper. A dat mi send you to school fa.' She doesn't say anything about school making her daughter stop speaking Creole. The answer therefore is option (C).

4. What feature of Caribbean English Creole grammar is exemplified in the expression 'Teacher mad!'?

   A. ~~Subject–verb agreement~~

   B. Zero-copula construction

   C. ~~Absence of tense marker~~

   D. Front-focusing

> You then have to try to remember what the two remaining options mean.
>
> Perhaps front-focusing doesn't sound right. (It refers to changing the order of words in a sentence so that what the speaker wants to emphasise is at the beginning of the sentence.)
>
> Perhaps you will remember that a copula is a verb, often the verb 'be', and that it links the subject ('Teacher' in the test item) and the predicate ('mad' in the test item). In a zero-copula construction the copula is missing.
>
> Obviously, it would be better if you knew this and could select the correct response straightaway.

> If you are unsure, eliminate those options that are obviously wrong first.
>
> There is no verb, so the issue cannot be about subject–verb agreement or tense marking.
>
> You can therefore eliminate options (A) and (C).

5. Which of the following does NOT reflect the phonology of Caribbean English Creole?

   A. 'Is a homework'

   B. ~~'Shet yu mout'~~

   C. ~~'get ahead wid dat'~~

   D. ~~'mi a go call yu mada'~~

> You didn't need the stimulus for this question so you should already have worked out the answer.

More worked examples

Step 1

Read the questions and options and underline the key terms and expressions in the questions.

6. Which types of communicative behaviour do the girls use to make Tori feel unwelcome?

   A. Body language and proxemics

   B. Proxemics and paralanguage

   C. Body language and artefacts

   D. Paralanguage and artefacts

> This test item requires that you not only know what is meant by 'communicative behaviour' but also know what the different communicative behaviours are.
>
> When you read the stimulus, you need to look out for which communicative behaviours are used.
>
> You also need to look at how they are used because the question asks which are used 'to make Tori feel unwelcome'.

7. Kyana's body language in Box 5 indicates that

   A. she finds the behaviour of her friends funny.

   B. she is hurt by her friends' actions.

   C. she empathises with Tori and is saddened by her friends' actions.

   D. she is angry with her friends and doesn't want to be their friend anymore.

> This test item is not asking you about Kyana's body language generally, it is specific to one box. Therefore in order to respond to this test item you will need to focus on that box – Box 5.

8. What kind of communication context is depicted in the scenario?

   A. Small group

   B. Intercultural

   C. Intrapersonal

   D. Interpersonal

> This item again tests your knowledge of the syllabus. You need to know what is meant by 'communication context'. Additionally you need to know what characterises each of the contexts given and what makes them different from each other.

9. What language function is performed through Ella's tweet?

   A. Communicating information

   B. Ridiculing someone

   C. Expressing feelings and emotions

   D. Recapturing experiences

> This item requires you to determine the communicative purpose of the information that Ella tweeted. You therefore need to be aware of the different functions of language, both verbal and non-verbal.
>
> The test item specifies Ella's tweet so to respond to this item you need to focus on the tweet in the scenario.

10. Which word below BEST sums up the tone of Ella's tweet?

   A. Angry

   B. Derisive

   C. Humorous

   D. Apprehensive

> This item is testing your comprehension and by extension your vocabulary.
>
> You should know that tone refers to how someone or something sounds or the manner in which something was said.
>
> You also need to know the meaning of each word in the options.
>
> To answer this item you could try reading the tweet aloud (but quietly).

Step 2

Study the stimulus on the next page. Underline the information in the stimulus that will help you answer the questions.

Instructions: Look carefully at the following scenario and then answer Items 6–10.

Step 3

Go back to the test items, re-read them and select your response.
Remember: If you do not know the answer or if you are unsure, use the
process of elimination.

6. Which types of communicative behaviour do the girls use to make Tori feel unwelcome?

   A. Body language and proxemics
   B. ~~Proxemics and paralanguage~~
   C. ~~Body language and artefacts~~
   D. ~~Paralanguage and artefacts~~

The remaining option and the correct response for the item is option (A).

You need to know what the various terms in the options mean.

The only example of paralanguage that is seen in this scenario is the emoji and this wasn't to make Tori feel unwelcome. You can therefore eliminate options (B) and (D).

No artefacts (i.e. objects) were used for this purpose either so option (C) can also be eliminated.

7. Kyana's body language in Box 5 indicates that
    A. she finds the behaviour of her friends funny.
    B. she is hurt by her friends' actions.
    C. she empathises with Tori and is saddened by her friends' actions.
    D. she is angry with her friends and doesn't want to be their friend anymore.

In Box 5, Kyana is looking away from her friends and looks upset.
Option (A) is contradicted by her body language so can be eliminated.

The tweet is not about her so *she* is not hurt by her friends' actions, so option (B) can be eliminated.

The correct response is therefore option (C).

There is no indication that she is angry or that she wants to disassociate from her friends, so option (D) can also be eliminated.

8. What kind of communication context is depicted in the scenario?
    A. Small group
    B. Intercultural
    C. Intrapersonal
    D. Interpersonal

Small group communication, option (B), is between individuals with shared beliefs and norms. It is often characterised by leadership. Ella, Kyla and Kyana could be said to form a group but Tori is not a part of it. Option (C) can therefore be eliminated.

Option (B) can be eliminated since there is no information to suggest that the speakers are from different cultural backgrounds.

Option (C) can be eliminated since this scenario is not about the communication of one of the individuals with herself.

The correct response is option (D).

Options (B) and (C) both seem to be good choices.

In a case such as this, go for the option which is more suitable.

Option (C) speaks directly to expressing feelings, which you might expect to see more typically in a diary perhaps.

The tweet seems to lean more towards making fun at Tori's expense and so option (B) is the better choice.

9. What language function is performed through Ella's tweet?
    A. Communicating information
    B. Ridiculing someone
    C. Expressing feelings and emotions
    D. Recapturing experiences

Using your knowledge of the syllabus, you can immediately eliminate options (A) and (D) as inappropriate.

Option (C) can also be eliminated because her word choice is not amusing.

10. Which word below BEST sums up the tone of Ella's tweet?
    A. Angry
    B. Derisive
    C. Humorous
    D. Apprehensive

Remember this test item is comprehension based so review the box that presents Ella's tweet (Box 5).

Because you are trying to determine how something sounds you need to focus on the words used.

Ella's word choice does not make her sound nervous, worried or uneasy so option (D) can be eliminated.

Angry is too strong an emotion in this instance so option (A) can be eliminated too.

'Derisive' means mocking, disdainful or scornful. This seems to be the emotion that reflects the manner in which Ella has tweeted based on the words used.

General pointers

Preparing for the exam

- KNOWLEDGE OF THE SYLLABUS CONTENT IS KEY.
    Study (and know) the definitions given in the syllabus.
    Learn the meaning of key terms.
    This, of course, is also vital for Section A.

- Practise answering multiple-choice questions.
    Establish a strategy to use in the exam.
    Perhaps the best is to answer the items you find easiest first. Then answer those you find more difficult and finally deal with those you find most difficult.
    Be sure to indicate which items you need to return to. (You could use an asterisk (*).)

There are exam-style multiple-choice questions relating to the different modules at the end of Chapters 2, 3 and 4 for you to practise with.

During the exam

- Be mindful of the time. (See section below.)
- The items in the exam are grouped and usually each group has a stimulus.

  Work on one group of items at a time.
- Read the items and options first and use the key words and expressions in them to inform your detailed reading of the stimulus they relate to.
- Make sure you answer **all** the items.

  When in doubt, use the process of elimination to help you work out the answer.
- Do not second-guess your choices. Only alter your selection if you are **absolutely certain** of the change you are about to make.

Time management

How well you manage your time on Paper 1 can be a key factor in your passing or failing (in addition to how well prepared you are, of course).

Remember the paper comprises two sections. You have 90 minutes to complete the entire paper once the examiner tells you to begin. The time starts after the extract for the listening comprehension has been read to you twice.

- You should aim to spend no more than 10 minutes on Section A.

  You have already been through the test items and heard the extract.

  Use three minutes to review your notes and the remaining seven minutes to answer the seven test items.
- **Do not** go on to Section B without completing Section A.

  If you do, you are likely to forget the extract and find it difficult to correctly complete the test items.
- Use the remaining 80 minutes for Section B.
- Timing is tricky because you will have around nine stimuli to read in addition to the 38 test items.

  The number of stimuli may vary and some will be longer than others.

  You will have (80 – 38) = 42 minutes available for reading.

  If there are nine stimuli, this means you have on average about four and a half minutes for Steps 1 and 2, i.e. reading each stimulus and the test items that go with it.

  When practising, work with this time in mind.

  Be aware, though, that some sections will take less time because the stimulus is shorter and some may take more time because the stimulus is longer.
- Do not spend more than one minute on any test item during Step 3, when you actually answer the question.

  If a test item proves too difficult, leave it and move on.

  You can always go back once you have completed the other, easier, test items.

Introduction

The idea for Module 1 is to give you the requisite skills to gather and process information. Gather in the sense that you know not only how to be discriminatory and how to identify and access valid and reliable data but also what note-taking skills to apply in collecting this data and methods to apply when attempting to source and collect it.

Gathering information is one thing but understanding what to do with it is another. In this regard the module enables you to decode and understand data that you have collected as well as data that is presented to you in the form of articles, essays, reports, etc. The aim of this module is to provide you with a set of skills – interpretive, analytical and writing, for instance – that you may apply to a body of information so that you may be able to use it coherently and logically. Also, a major part of this two-pronged module is the development of your comprehension skills, which are critical for your success, not just in this course but throughout life. Essentially, the module prepares you for conducting research, which will be an integral aspect of your academic life.

Exam Tip

For Paper 2 item 1, you will be given an extract from an article, speech, report or other text.

The extract may be any one of the discourse types:

- Narrative
- Descriptive
- Expository
- Persuasive
- Argumentative

It is important to identify the discourse type as this will help you in identifying the language strategies and/or techniques used as well as the organisational strategies.

Discourse types

This section will remind you of the characteristic formats, organisational features and modes of expression of different genres and types of writing and speech.

There are two major classifications of discourse.

- **Artistic discourse**
  This includes creative writing such as novels, stories and poetry and also personal accounts such as biographies and journals. This type of writing focuses on expressing the author's thoughts and ideas through their imagination. The emphasis is on the author's feelings and emotions as opposed to facts.

Objectives

This chapter will help you revise these objectives:

- identify the characteristic formats, organisational features and modes of expression of different genres and types of writing and speech;

- apply any of the different levels of comprehension to examples of spoken and written material;

- write continuous prose and note-form summaries of specific types of written and spoken material;

- determine the appropriateness of data collection methods and instruments, including the use of the Internet as an electronic resource;

- evaluate the effect of primary and secondary sources, context and medium (or channel) on the reliability and validity of information.

Exam Tip

Module 1 content prepares you to respond to the first 15 multiple-choice items on Paper 1 and to item 1 on Paper 2.

- **Technical or scientific discourse**

  With this kind of discourse the author is generally writing about a specialised or particular subject area. This generally requires direction, instruction or explanation and often uses specialised terms and expressions. This type of writing tends to be highly factual and evidence driven.

  Despite being classified as artistic discourse, persuasive texts may share many of the features of technical or scientific discourse, particularly of argumentative texts. The main difference is that an argumentative piece is neutral, although it may attempt to prove that one viewpoint is correct, whereas a persuasive piece seeks to make the audience take some action and it may therefore be biased. In order to achieve its aim of persuading the audience to action, it may use language techniques more often found in artistic discourse.

  With technical writing there is a lot of emphasis on the writer's diction (specificity of word choice) and with artistic writing the focus is largely on the writer's tone or the overall effect conveyed by the word choice.

Comparison of technical or scientific discourse and artistic discourse

Technical or scientific discourse	Artistic discourse
Objective	Subjective
Evidence based	Opinions, biases
Denotative/concrete words	Connotative words
Precise language	Figurative language
Neutral tone	Affective tone
Discourse types:	**Discourse types:**
Expository	Narrative
Argumentative	Descriptive
	Persuasive

A piece of writing or speech may contain more than one discourse type. For example, stories may contain both narrative and descriptive text.

The table gives a comparison of the different types of discourse, but be aware that there are always exceptions.

Comparison of the different types of discourse

Discourse type	Formats	Purpose	Organisational features*	Modes of expression*
Narrative	Novels Short stories Anecdotes Autobiographies	To entertain To explain To recount or relate an experience To highlight	Flashback Flash-forward Foreshadowing Time sequence	Descriptive language Figurative language and literary devices Conversational tone Dialogue Voice/narrative perspective
Descriptive	Journals Poetry Stories Biographies	To entertain To illustrate To explain To describe To visually present To invent To expose To highlight	Comparison Contrast Description General to specific Spatial order Time sequence	Descriptive language Figurative language and literary devices Anecdotes

* See later for more on organisational features and modes of expression.

Discourse type	Formats	Purpose	Organisational features*	Modes of expression*
Expository *Text is objective and impartial. It is balanced and factual.*	Reports News articles Academic writing How-to (process) essays Instructions Directions	To illustrate or demonstrate To prove To explain, teach or instruct To inform, reveal or expose To declare To chronicle To alert or caution To establish	Cause and effect Classification Comparison and contrast Definitions Evidence Illustrations and examples Problem and solution	Objective arguments Precise language Neutral tone Presentation of evidence
Argumentative *Text is objective but may aim to demonstrate the superiority of one position over another through balanced argument.*	Critical review Letters of recommendation Letters to the editor Editorials Debates	To prove the validity of an idea To convince To influence	Comparison and contrast Counterarguments Concession and rebuttal Evidence Illustrations and examples Lists Reasons Refutations	Objective arguments Precise language Use of logos Neutral tone Presentation of evidence
Persuasive *Text may be subjective and partial. It is often biased in favour of a particular position.*	Opinion pieces Commentaries Speeches Advertisements	To urge the audience to take action To convince To complain To criticise To influence	Cause and effect Counterarguments Concession and rebuttal Evidence Illustrations and examples Lists Order of importance Problem and solution Reasons Refutations	Lack of objectivity Use of pathos Non-neutral tone Presentation of evidence Rhetorical questions Restatement and reiteration List of three Anecdotes

Organisational features of narrative and descriptive discourse

Flashback

A flashback is an episode that took place in a time earlier than the present action.

It may be used for different purposes: to increase tension, to move the story forward by providing relevant back-story, to provide a context to current events, to give background to explain a conflict, to provide insight into a character's motives, etc.

Flashbacks are often presented through dream sequences (the character falls asleep and dreams about past events or occurrences) and memories (the character may see or hear or feel something and it interrupts his/her present musings and takes him/her back to a past moment).

Flashbacks can also be presented in a straightforward fashion so the author will indicate that he/she is going back in time.

For example: *Jonathan thought of last year's charity gala and the disaster it turned out to be and there and then the whole horrid affair flooded his consciousness. It was Thursday night. Late. About 11:40 p.m. or so. He walked into the town hall …*

Exam Tip

Although the different types of discourse tend to have characteristic organisational features and modes of expression you need to be able to recognise them even when they occur in types of discourse where you wouldn't usually expect them.

Exam Tip

Understanding why an author uses flashback will help you to explain its use and effectiveness in a piece of writing.

Flash-forward

This strategy is opposite to flashback in that it takes the narrative forward in time from the current time in the sequence of events being presented. The author interrupts the current flow of events to insert an event that will take place at some future time.

Flash-forward can be used to create momentum in a narrative as well as motivation for driving plot and can help readers understand the significance of characters' actions.

Foreshadowing

This is a hint that an author gives in advance of what is to come in the narrative.

This can be done through the characters' dialogue or given through the title of the text or a chapter in the narrative.

Authors use foreshadowing to create suspense and it therefore adds dramatic tension in the narrative as it has readers anticipating what is going to happen next. It may also assist readers in comprehending later outcomes in a narrative.

Time sequence

Much artistic discourse uses time sequencing as an organisational strategy. Often this is chronological. A narrative discourse often has an initiating event, problems and complications that build to the climax, then the strands of the plot are worked out, leading to a resolution.

Authors will use chronological order to help the audience to understand the relationship between the causes and effects of events. This way the audience will be able to rationalise why things happen in the way they do.

Comparison

This is a description that focuses on the similarity between two or more things, ideas or individuals.

An author may use comparison in order to emphasise a quality or make the quality more vivid in the minds of the audience.

The author may present the comparison using various literary devices such as metaphor, simile, analogy or even personification.

Comparisons tend to capture the audience's attention and make it easier for them to understand concepts, because the comparisons used are general ones taken from real life.

Contrast

This is the opposite to comparison as it focuses on the differences between two or more things, ideas or individuals.

An author may use this strategy in order to make a concept clearer to readers. It strengthens the author's argument and therefore makes it stand out more in the minds of the audience. Naturally this is done with the author's purpose in mind.

Description

Description uses sensory details to portray a person, place, thing or even an idea or concept. What it does is create images in the audience's minds. This makes it easier to recall.

As images tend to have more influence on people's thoughts, this may cause them to lean towards the author's bias, according to his/her purpose.

General to specific

With this method of organisation the author moves from broad observations on the topic to giving more specific details.

Authors tend to use this strategy to focus on important details.

Spatial order

In this kind of description, the information on items is presented according to their physical position in relation to each other or according to their location in space.

Organisational features of expository, argumentative and persuasive discourse

Cause and effect

The author presents information to explain the reason something happens – the cause, and what happens because of it – the effect.

This strategy helps the reader make a connection between action and consequences or understand the relationship between two things.

Classification

The author arranges or groups ideas, information or things according to shared characteristics or similarities so that it is ordered into categories.

For instance, natural disasters may be classified according to types.

Comparison and contrast

Throughout the discourse the author highlights the similarities and differences between two or more things, ideas or individuals.

Concession and rebuttal

The author acknowledges a point or argument that opposes the position he/she is presenting (concession) before proving it wrong (rebuttal).

By acknowledging the point or argument the author shows he/she understands the other position and is somewhat unbiased but at the same time his/her rebuttal discredits that very position as it attacks the point that he/she just acknowledged.

This shows the audience that the opposing argument is weak and invalid and highlights the author's argument as being more acceptable.

Counterarguments

Similar to concession and rebuttal, counterarguments make allowances for the opposite perspective. The difference is that a counterargument is an objection to an objection.

This means that in presenting his/her argument, the author may indicate that people holding opposing views may have an objection to it. The author outlines this objection and immediately refutes that objection by presenting a new argument that opposes the objection raised – that is, the counterargument.

Be mindful that a counterargument has two features – the objection and a rejection of the objection.

What the counterargument does is contradict the objection raised and support this with evidence or reasoning. It encourages the audience to dismiss objection as invalid and accept the counter argument presented.

Definitions

The author explains the meaning of a concept, idea or thing or clarifies a concept, idea or thing by explaining what it is or what it represents.

Evidence

The author presents facts and data to prove or disprove something or to substantiate and strengthen claims made by the author.

Evidence may be in the form of facts, statistical or historical data, testimony, quotes from reputable sources and even logics.

Evidence adds credibility to an argument, thus increasing the chances of the audience trusting the claim made.

Illustrations and examples

The author makes an idea clearer by providing illustrations and examples. These provide further evidence and support for an argument. They might help explain a concept or give details in the form of examples that will prove a theory.

For example, in order to prove that hurricanes are dangerous, the author may illustrate this statement by identifying past hurricanes and giving examples of the damage that they caused.

Juxtaposition

Used mainly in argumentative and persuasive discourse, the author will often juxtapose a conflicting argument or statement with a counterargument in order to strengthen his claim.

This will be done in a bid to discredit the other side of the argument while at the same time presenting the writer as thoughtful and well-reasoned. This tends to make the author's claims more acceptable to the audience.

Lists

The author provides a series of details, facts or images.

This helps to add to the general mood of the piece and brings across factual information clearly and succinctly. It therefore brings clarity to the author's argument and allows the audience to follow his/her line of reasoning to its conclusion.

Order of importance

The author presents and develops his/her points based on their level of importance.

The ideas are often presented from most important to least but the reverse order may also be used.

Problem and solution

The author presents a problem, details the specifics of the problem (i.e. the problem is explained) and then gives an outline as to how the problem can be solved.

Reasons

The author rationalises a point of view by outlining causes, justifications or explanations.

This often creates empathy and leads the audience to believe that the argument's end point is a logical conclusion.

Exam Tip

It is important to assess the reliability and validity of the evidence presented by the author.

See page 36 for more on this.

Refutations

The author argues against a particular position. He/she identifies the mistake or weakness in an argument and presents reasoning to indicate why the conclusions or reasons are mistaken, flawed, weak or wrong.

Modes of expression of narrative and descriptive discourse

Modes of expression refer to the various ways in which the author expresses his/her ideas, his/her language style and the techniques and strategies he/she uses.

Descriptive language

The author uses descriptive language to help the audience build impressions and images in their minds and to keep them engaged in the piece.

Words can have both a denotative (dictionary) and a connotative (associated) meaning. Authors of artistic discourse choose the words they use very carefully to create the mood, tone and atmosphere they want to convey. The words used can also convey the author's attitude to his/her subject as well as influence the audience's feelings towards the subject.

Authors use words to help the audience to hear, taste, feel, see and smell the people, places and things described in the text and make them seem real and believable. The images created help give the audience a better understanding of characters and their situation, especially the hero and villain.

Adjectives, adverbs and vivid verbs are instrumental in descriptive language as they help to add life to what is being described.

- **Adjectives**
  Specific and descriptive adjectives enhance a description, helping to paint a better picture of the person, event, incident or thing being described.

- **Adverbs**
  Adverbs add further colour to the description as they give greater detail about how something was done or when. They make the piece more vivid and the images easier to visualise.

- **Vivid verbs**
  Authors will choose verbs that clearly create an image of what is happening so the audience can better picture the action and be drawn into it.
  For instance, instead of saying 'Tom walked into the house', 'walk' may be replaced by a verb that highlights his exact movements, e.g. 'stumbled', 'crawled', 'limped', 'skipped', 'sauntered'. Each of these alternatives show a clear movement but they also convey other ideas. They suggest Tom's likely mood and/or condition.

Figurative language and literary devices

Figurative language is the use of words or expressions to convey meaning in ways which may be outside of their literal meanings.

Literary devices use words in a particular way to create an effect.

Figurative language and literary devices make the piece more interesting and dramatic and help paint pictures in the minds of the

Exam Tip

Figurative language and literary devices are used to create an effect.

You need to say what this effect is.

Exam Tip

Make sure you are able
to identify these language
techniques so you can
respond effectively to test
item 1 on Paper 2.

audience. As with descriptive language, the author chooses the words he/
she uses very carefully to suit his/her purpose.

- **Alliteration**
  The occurrence of the same consonant sound at the beginning of
  adjacent or closely connected words.
  Example: 'I savour the song sounding sweetly in my ears.'

- **Allusion**
  An expression designed to call something to mind without mentioning
  it explicitly; an indirect or passing reference.
  Example: '… and so he struts around, poised and pampered like the
  prodigal son …'
  'prodigal son' is an allusion to a biblical story. It relies on the audience
  knowing the story so they can build a picture of the man's behaviour.

- **Analogy**
  A comparison between one thing and another, typically for the
  purpose of explanation or clarification.
  Example: 'If you want to understand how meaningful it is to feed
  your brain well, think of what happens when you feed garbage to
  your CPU.'

- **Assonance**
  The repetition of similar vowel sounds occurring in words that are
  close together.
  Example: The bad cad was a sad lad.

- **Euphemism**
  The use of a milder, softer or more acceptable expression or
  description in place of one which may be impolite or insensitive.
  Authors use euphemistic expressions to reduce the harshness. Often
  authors use euphemism to write about topics that are social taboo. It
  tends to make certain topics more acceptable and polite.
  Example: 'My grandfather is **no longer with us**.'
  'No longer with us' is a euphemism for 'dead'.

- **Hyperbole**
  An exaggeration made in order to create a desired effect. This is
  generally to make something (a situation, condition or individual)
  appear, for example, bigger or better or worse or more grandiose than
  it actually is.
  Authors use it for emphasis. It may be used to create humour or
  emotional impact.
  Example: 'I run faster than the speed of light, faster than even Bolt.'

- **Irony**
  Using words in such a way that the intended or implied meaning of
  the words used is different from the actual meaning.
  It also speaks to a situation in which the opposite of what is
  expected to happen actually happens or the result of a situation is the
  opposite of what is anticipated.
  Irony can help the audience to see deeper meanings in things
  expressed.
  Examples: **Situational irony** –'Isabelle left her umbrella at home for
  the first time in weeks because there had consistently been no rain
  and, for the first time in weeks, it rained.'

Verbal irony – 'As the rain soaks through Isabelle's uniform she mutters, "Perfect! What a great way to have a bath. Bring it on universe!"'

- **Litotes**
  A form of understatement used for emphasis by stating the negative in order to highlight or affirm the positive.
  Example: Your friend gave a speech and did it very well. After the speech, in congratulating him you say, "that wasn't bad", meaning he did well.

- **Metaphor**
  A comparative technique that presents the likeness between two things by saying one is the other. With metaphors, comparisons are implied rather than stated.
  Example: 'My mum is a rock in my life.'

- **Onomatopoeia**
  The use of a word which imitates the sound it represents.
  Examples: hiss, fizz, bang.

- **Oxymoron**
  The use of two contrasting terms to create an effect which is usually dramatic or comical. Usually it is a combination of an adjective and a noun.
  In addition to creating a dramatic or comical effect, an oxymoron may provoke the audience to think about the phrase used and engage in some kind of analysis to decipher the meaning of it.
  Examples: honest lies, serious joke, painfully sweet (memories).
  Sometimes the oxymoron is separated by intervening phrases, for instance, 'to learn to win is to learn to lose'.

- **Paradox**
  A seemingly self-contradictory statement that conveys a truth. It is often used to invite the audience to think outside the box. It sometimes conveys a level of irony that engenders thought and may elicit a greater interest in the subject matter.
  Example: 'It's a pity that youth is wasted on the very young.' – George Bernard Shaw.

- **Pathetic fallacy**
  This is where aspects of nature are given human feelings or emotions. For example: The **melancholy** weather dampened the atmosphere.
  Hurricane Izzy was not **afraid** to spew her **outrage**.
  The words in bold are all human emotions or feelings.
  Pathetic fallacy is a type of personification because it is the attribution of human characteristics but note carefully that it is specific in that it is the giving of human emotions or feelings to *elements of nature*.
  Personification is broader. It deals with a wide range of human characteristics, not just feelings, and to all non-human things, not just elements of nature.

- **Personification**
  A device used for comparison. Personification works by giving human characteristics to inanimate objects, ideas or animals so conveying the idea that this non-human entity has the ability to act according to the human characteristics assigned to it.
  Example: 'The wind whispered its secrets in the forest.'

Note

Paradox and oxymoron may seem similar but they are very different.

An oxymoron contains two contrasting terms, whilst a paradox is a statement (which can be one or even several sentences) which appears contradictory but may be true.

Note

Remember: **person**ification – having characteristics of a **person**.

It is not to be confused with metaphor, which in making a comparison can sometimes resemble personification.

- **Pun**
  This is the intentional use of a word with two or more meanings or words that sound similar to create a desired effect, usually one of humour.

  Puns add humour and meaning to a text and also influence the audience's interpretation of the text.

  Examples: 'I was struggling to figure out how lightning works, then it struck me'; 'Why can't a bicycle stand up? Because it's two-tyred.'

- **Sarcasm**
  This is where the literal meaning of what is said or written is different from what the author intends to communicate.

  The aim of sarcasm is to mock or hurt the person, group, institution or society at which the piece is directed.

  Example: 'Well done, well done, mr politician man / U done wonderful job a tear down we country demolition man / Well done, well done, mr politician man / U done such a great job a sellin out we country wid u business plan / U fi get a round of applause / Fi all the work u doin / Decisions weh u mek weh lef di country inna ruins yo' – extract from the lyrics of Kabaka Pyramid's 'Well Done', written by Luana Grandani.

- **Satire**
  Satire uses humour, irony, exaggeration and ridicule to comment on a serious matter in a way that is funny. Many comedians use satire in talking about serious issues that affect society.

  Authors use satire to expose and criticise foolishness or corruption of an individual or a society. Satire highlights problems so as to expose them and bring them to the forefront of the audience's consciousness.

  Satire is found in many political cartoons and also in books and plays, for example, Patrick Brown's *Breadfruit Kingdom*.

- **Simile**
  A comparison using expressions such as 'as' or 'like'. This is a direct comparison, unlike a metaphor.

  Authors use a simile to compare two different things that they believe are alike.

  Example: 'I clung tight like a lizard to a branch.'

- **Synecdoche**
  A figure of speech in which a part is substituted for a whole or a whole is substituted for a part.

  Examples: 'He had some cool new wheels'; 'Jamaica took six gold medals at the 2016 Olympics.'

- **Tautology**
  The repetition of an idea using different words.

  Example: 'We **take our last breath** and we **die**.'

Conversational tone

Narrative writing will often have a conversational tone, an informal or friendly means of speaking. It comes across as natural because the author writes in the way in which one would generally speak. It creates the sense that the audience is directly involved in the narrative and/or that the author is speaking directly to the audience.

To make the narrative conversational, the author may use more contractions, shorter sentences and may even start sentences with conjunctions or end them with prepositions. The author may use slang or colloquialisms. The author may also use a lot of personal pronouns to make the narrative at once relatable and engaging.

Authors may choose this mode as it is easier to understand, helps to build credibility and also builds rapport with the audience. It is a good way of achieving this purpose.

Dialogue

Dialogue is a conversation between two or more people.

It may be used in narrative discourse not only to move the story along, and faster, but also to help you to understand the characters. Dialogue also tends to create interest in the narrative. Because dialogue gives voice to the characters it is one way in which the author pulls the audience into the story and allows them to follow the evolution of the characters, which help them to better understand the story as a whole.

Voice/narrative perspective

When creating a narrative, the author needs to decide who is telling the story or from whose point of view the story is told. The point of view used helps to control how the audience will receive the story. The narrative perspective used influences the impressions the audience forms and the conclusions they draw from the plot. Authors tend to use one of three points of view.

- **First person**
  The person telling the story is a character in the story. He/she has an active role (sometimes the protagonist) in the unfolding of the plot. The pronouns 'I' and 'we' are used when stories are narrated in first person. This point of view shares the inner thoughts of the character with the audience and so they are generally more empathetic towards him/her.

- **Third person limited**
  The narrator has an all-knowing role, however the story is told through one single character. This means that the narrator knows the thoughts and feelings of only one character, who is followed throughout the story. In narrating events, the pronouns 'she', 'he' and 'it' are used.

- **Third person omniscient**
  The narrator has an all-knowing role. He/she is not involved in the narrative but has an overview of everything that goes on in the story. This allows him/her to move between events and to know all the characters' actions and feelings.

  Although the third person omniscient presents the audience with multiple viewpoints, it can remove the urgency from the narrative and makes it less relatable.

Anecdotes

Anecdotes are short, generally amusing or interesting stories that are based on facts that are used to tell readers about an event or incident that happened in the past.

Often authors will include anecdotes to assist in communicating the point of the discourse. It may be a personal anecdote or it may be just a story that helps to relate a relevant idea. The objective is that it should help the audience get a better understanding of what is being presented in the discourse. It helps the discourse as it adds a human quality and provides insights into the situation being presented that might not have been conveyed any other way.

Modes of expression of expository, argumentative and persuasive discourse

Objective arguments

The information and arguments presented in expository and argumentative discourse are based on facts. They are free of bias.

In argumentative texts, the audience should be able to see all aspects of the argument and be able to form their own conclusions even though the author's purpose may be to convince them that a particular position is superior.

Lack of objectivity

Persuasive discourse may be biased. The text may reflect the author's personal feelings and opinions. The author may not present all sides of the argument or he/she may attempt to influence the audience to accept his/her position.

Precise language

In expository and argumentative discourse the author aims to make the information and arguments presented clear and accessible. Authors are likely to use the denotative (dictionary) meaning of words and avoid figurative language.

Authors of persuasive discourse may also use precise language so that the audience can follow their arguments.

- **Technical terms and jargon**

  Authors will tailor the language they use to their audience. An author addressing the general public would tend to avoid using technical terms and jargon as they may not be understood. However, an author addressing an audience working in his/her field would use them. Technical terms and jargon are content specific and allow the author to present information and arguments with precision and economy of expression.

  An author using technical terms and jargon when addressing the general public may be attempting to make himself/herself appear authoritative.

- **Logical linkages**

  These are transitional words and phrases that help to establish logical connections and relationships between ideas and also between paragraphs or sections of the text.

  Authors use these to help the audience understand the information and follow the argument more easily.

  (See Chapter 5 for more details and examples.)

Use of logos and neutral tone

Authors of expository and argumentative discourse use logos and a neutral tone.
- When authors use logos they are appealing to logic.
- They use rational arguments when presenting their claims.
- Claims are supported by evidence and reasoning.
- A fallacy is an incorrect or misleading statement based on inaccurate facts or faulty reasoning. An author may point out a fallacy in an argument put forward by somebody with an opposing view.

Exam Tip

Although argumentative and persuasive discourse are similar, they are not the same. In persuasive discourse, the author's aim is to take a stand and persuade the audience to accept it; in argumentative discourse the author's aim is to argue a position, proving to the audience why he/she agrees or disagrees with the position.

- They use a neutral tone to present information and the audience has to think in order to assess the information.

Use of pathos and non-neutral tone

Authors of persuasive discourse may use pathos and a non-neutral tone.
- When authors use pathos they are appealing to emotions.
- Authors use emotive language and their aim is to convince the audience to accept their arguments by eliciting an emotional response, such as anger, pity, fear, sorrow, patriotism or empathy.
- They may use a passionate tone to demonstrate that they are convinced of the correctness of their point of view.
- They may use inclusive language to give the impression that they are talking from the audience's point of view.
- They are more likely to use figurative language and literary devices, such as hyperbole and litotes, to make their arguments more persuasive.

Presentation of evidence

- **Facts**
  Authors use facts (i.e. information that has been accepted as true and that is able to withstand scrutiny) as evidence to support their points and arguments.
  Facts add credibility to the piece and give it greater authenticity.
  The audience is more likely to believe an author who uses facts than one who doesn't.

- **Statistical or historical data**
  Authors use numerical data to substantiate the claims they put forward.
  Again, this adds credibility and so is used by authors to prompt you to accept what they are presenting as acceptable.

- **Expert opinion**
  Although expert opinions are based on factual evidence they may not be counted as fact because they are the conclusions drawn by individuals, albeit those who may be considered an authority on the matter.
  Generally people are more trusting when information comes from a source of authority.
  Expert opinion is, therefore, another way to add credibility to the claims and arguments being made by the author.

Rhetorical questions

Rhetorical questions are used for dramatic effect. They are attention grabbing.
  They invite the audience to think but they can also invite the audience to share the author's opinion.

Restatement and reiteration

At some later point in his/her writing or speech, the author repeats an earlier idea without changing the wording – restatement, or alludes to an idea presented earlier – reiteration.
  These strategies are used largely for emphasis. They help to clarify the author's argument or point of view and make it stand out so much in the audience's minds that they are encouraged to accept it.

Exam Tip

Rhetorical questions, restatement and reiteration are powerful persuasive devices. However, authors of argumentative texts may also use these devices in conjunction with logical arguments to convince the audience of their points of view.

List of three

Lists are used to show that there are a number of examples and to demonstrate range and variety, but they also reinforce an idea.

A list of three creates rhythm without the text, making it particularly powerful. It is a device very often used in political speeches.

Anecdotes

See also page 27.

Authors of persuasive discourse may use anecdotes to help the audience identify with them.

Example of an argumentative text

Clear statement using precise language and a neutral tone. It begins with a statement that not only introduces the subject of the argument but also gives a reason for the author's support of the argument.

Evidence from a reliable source is quoted.

The student exchange programme to Australia is a constructive way for me to spend my vacation this summer. I will be among the 75% of the student population that benefits every year from going to different countries to learn about their cultures, studying with different lecturers and participating in research work that benefits their continued studies. The records from the National Education Association and from the Ministry of Education show that these students perform better and are more socially and culturally adjusted than students who do not participate in the programme. Furthermore, going on the exchange programme will earn me two extra credits.

List of benefits shows range and variety. (Note that there are three benefits given.)

Additional reason given so that text ends with a statement that further reinforces the author's support for the argument.

Example of a persuasive text

Short opening sentence to create drama.

List of three emotive words to influence the audience's feelings.

Emotive language to create a sense of outrage in the audience.

Reiteration of the author's opinion of the criminal.

Use of the personal pronoun 'our' encourages the audience to believe that the author is speaking on their behalf.

He took the lives of twenty-five victims. Twenty-five innocent, helpless, promising young women. Ripped away their innocence, slashed their throats and sent blood-written postcards to family members. After each gruesome act he went home, turned on his television and continued with life like a normal human being while the families were left devastated by each senseless tragedy. Yet, his well-paid team of lawyers want you well-meaning, God-fearing, honest jurors to believe that this heartless, psychopathic monster, who feels no remorse, deserves to live. Think of your daughters, sisters, nieces. Think of the twenty-five he mercilessly murdered. It is clear. How can spending our hard-earned taxes to keep him in prison possibly be justice? The death sentence is the only just punishment.

Repetition of the number to show the enormity of the crime.

Use of metaphor to create an image of how callous the criminal is.

List of three adjectives adds power to the description by emphasising that the man in question is remorseless and cruel.

Rhetorical question encourages the audience to share the author's point of view.

Tone

- Every time you speak or write you convey a particular tone – a sound in your voice or a mood in your writing.
- Tone represents the author's attitude – to the subject of the discourse or to the audience.
- In artistic discourse especially, tone is used to convey mood.
- Tone is reflected in the word choices the author makes.
- It is also reflected in a speaker's tone of voice.
- It may also be reflected in a speaker's body language.

Some examples of tone

Amused	Critical	Passionate
Annoyed	Dark	Passive
Apathetic	Disdainful	Pleasant
Appreciative	Disgruntled	Questioning
Angry	Disgusted	Resigned
Authoritative	Facetious	Reverent
Belligerent	Flippant	Sad
Bitter	Formal	Sarcastic
Candid	Frivolous	Sardonic
Casual	Grave	Satirical
Ceremonial	Harsh	Sentimental
Cheerful	Hopeful	Serious
Comic	Impassioned	Solemn
Compassionate	Indignant	Sombre
Condescending	Ironic	Taunting
Confused	Irreverent	Unemotional
Contemptuous	Matter-of-fact	Urgent
Conversational	Nostalgic	Wry

Naturally, since the tone is linked to the subject matter it means that different pieces of writing or speech will employ different tones.

Also remember that tone is connected to the author's purpose.

When you are asked to comment on an author's tone you are being asked to identify their attitude based on what they have written. You may also need to express whether the tone is appropriate or not based on the context, the audience or even the purpose.

When you are producing different types of discourse you need to think about the situation and the words you will use for that situation.

If you are addressing your classmates about supporting an upcoming football match, for instance, the words and sentence structure you use will be different from what you would use to address the members of the school board and administrators in seeking their support of the same venture. You may use slang and casual forms of speech with your classmates but with the board members and administrators you would be more formal.

Similarly, in writing your valedictorian address for your graduation you may incorporate anecdotes of your past years that are funny and familiar yet still formal in the way they are expressed.

An academic paper or personal essay for a scholarship application is very different. In such writing you would want to remain interesting but definitely not frivolous or ignorant and so you would abstain from using casual language, slang and certain personal anecdotes.

Exam Tip

Think about how you sound when you are angry or sad or confused or annoyed or disgusted. Then think about the words you would choose to use in those different frames of mind. This should help you to think about tone.

Exam Tip

A piece of writing may have several tones.

Worked example

Identify the tone and comment on its appropriateness in this piece of writing.

Wow! I spent thousands of irretrievable hours, hours I could have spent at the mall or the movies, crafting the perfect volcano for my science project, even to the point of ensuring that it erupts just so, and all I get is a 'Well done, Bethany'. Isn't that just fifty shades of freaking awesome! What am I supposed to do with a 'Well done'? Thank you very much Miss continue-to-make-my-life-suck Francis.

The author's tone may be described as bitterly sarcastic and she is clearly indignant at what she perceives as an unjust response to her efforts. It is clear that she is not satisfied with the comment she received by the use of 'all I get', suggesting that it is highly insufficient for the 'thousands of hours' expended.

The language is very casual, suggesting that the audience is very familiar, maybe the author is addressing her friends or maybe even speaking to herself. In this case the tone is appropriate based on context and audience.

This bitterly sarcastic tone is appropriate to the content because the student is reflecting on an episode where she felt she was unfairly treated.

Levels of comprehension

This section will remind you how to apply the different levels of comprehension to examples of spoken and written material.

Comprehension skills enable you to process information that you have read or heard and to understand the meaning of it.

Understanding information occurs at different levels and being able to function at these various levels is important as it affects how well you perform, not only in Communication Studies but also in other subject areas.

Comprehension skills

These include the ability to:
- categorise and classify;
- compare and contrast;
- identify cause and effect;
- note details;
- recognise literary genres, organising strategies and language devices;
- separate facts and opinions;
- sequence events;
- use context clues.

Literal

- At this level you are required to understand what the text actually says.
- Answers to questions based on the literal level of understanding can be found in the text; it therefore deals with understanding and absorbing facts.
- It allows you to answer questions which ask 'who', 'what', 'when', 'where'.
- Your understanding at this level is the foundation for the higher-order comprehension skills.
- If you respond at the literal level you need to be able to:
  - summarise the main idea;
  - understand facts and data given in the text;
  - sequence events;
  - identify characters in a story and the relationships between them;
  - identify settings.

Interpretative

- At this level of comprehension you are required to 'read between the lines'. The focus is on what the author meant by what he said.
- You will need to build on your understanding of the facts in the text and use that to determine the deeper meaning behind the stated information.
- You will need to use evidence from the text and your reasoning ability to draw conclusions.
- Questions that require you to process at this level will often require you to supply examples from the text to support your responses.
- It allows you to answer questions which ask 'what if', 'why', 'how'.
- If you respond at the interpretative level you need to be able to:
  - make predictions;
  - make inferences;
  - identify the main idea when it is not explicitly stated;
  - identify the author's purpose;
  - recognise cause and effect relationships;
  - recognise tone and mood;
  - identify the theme.

Evaluative

- At this level of comprehension you are required to analyse the text and form an opinion based on the information given.
- At this level you are thinking critically about everything in the text as you are required to make a value judgement about an aspect of the text (an issue, idea, character or even the author himself/herself).
- It allows you to answer questions which ask 'why is something important?', 'how does something relate to real life?'.
- If you respond at the evaluative level you need to be able to:
  - consider the significance of actions, ideas or attitudes;
  - explain your position in response to information from the text;
  - make generalisations about the text;
  - consider underlying implications.

Applied

- At this level of comprehension you are required to analyse the text and go on to apply the information in the text to real-life situations.
- You need to make a connection between what you have read or heard and what you already know or believe.
- Your response will be based on the author's language, style, purpose, imagery and values. You need to merge what you understood at the literal and interpretative levels and extend these concepts beyond the situation.
- You will need to support your responses with logic or reason.
- It allows you to answer questions such as 'if you were ...', 'in what ways' or 'if these are ...' to list a few.
- If you respond at the applied level you need to be able to:
  - focus on translating topics into real-world situations;
  - create something original based on your response to the text.

Writing summaries

This section will remind you how to write continuous prose and note-form summaries.

It is important for you to remember that in order to write a good summary you must first understand the material that you read.

The information in the preceding section should help you to refine your comprehension skills.

Before writing a summary

- Scan the text to get a basic understanding.
  Take note of subheadings or how the text is divided into paragraphs.
  Identify the discourse type.

- Read the text in detail.
  Highlight or underline the main idea in each paragraph.
  Make notes in the margin of supporting details.

- Review the highlighted sections and notes.
- Rewrite the main idea in your own words.
- Review the supporting details.
  Check to ensure you have not included any minor details (things irrelevant to the text as a whole).
  Attempt to combine longer phrases into single words or much shorter phrases.

Writing the summary

- Review all the information you have written in your own words then combine it all using continuous prose or in note form.
- The first sentence should introduce the author and title of the piece.
- Maintain the same chronological order as the text.
- Ensure that you maintain the same tone and perspective as the author and that you have given an accurate and balanced account of what it represents.

Features of a summary

- A summary represents the text as a whole.
- It is not prejudiced by your biases (your opinions of the content).
- It is a shortened version of the whole.
- It should be presented in your own words.
- It must acknowledge the original source.

Things to leave out of a summary

- Examples
- Statistical data
- Repetitions
- Figures of speech
- Rhetorical questions
- Opinions

Data collection methods and instruments

This section will remind you how to determine the appropriateness of data collection methods and instruments.

Data can be divided into two types: primary and secondary.

- **Primary data**
  This is data that you collect yourself.

- **Secondary data**
  This is data collected by somebody else.

Methods of collecting primary data include:

- questionnaires;
- interviews;
- observation.

In deciding whether a data collection method is appropriate you will need to focus on its strengths and weaknesses.

Questionnaires

- Used when numerical data is required.
- The results can be analysed statistically.
- Questionnaires can provide factual information, for example, about how much a person spends on cosmetics.
- Questionnaires can also provide information about attitudes and feelings through the use of attitude and sentiment scales, for example: On a scale from 1 (agree strongly) to 5 (disagree strongly), how much do you agree with the statement …
- Questionnaires can be administered:
  - in person;
  - via the telephone;
  - via the postal mail;
  - via electronic mail.

Strengths

- Allow data to be collected from a large sample
- Easily administered
- Easily and reliably scored
- Allow for anonymity

Weaknesses

- Limited scope for probing responses
- Inflexibility
- Responses can be misleading
- Limitations can be posed by the literacy of the respondents
- Respondents' cooperation is imperative

Interviews

- Used when non-numerical data is required.
- Usually administered to the respondent face-to-face.
- Can either be structured or unstructured.
- Structured interviews use a set of precisely formulated questions.
- Unstructured interviews are very informal. They allow the respondents to speak for as long as they want in response to a stimulus question. Follow-up questions are determined by what the respondents say.

Strengths

- Yield in-depth information
- Allow the researcher more flexibility
- Can yield a lot of data
- Responses can be clarified

Exam Tip

Remember that the data collection method(s) you choose and the instruments you use to collect your data are dependent on the type of research you are doing. Most of the research you would have been doing, especially for your Internal Assessment portfolio, would be social surveys.

Weaknesses

- Time-consuming
- Samples are often quite small
- Can yield a lot of irrelevant data
- Can be affected by the researcher's biases
- The respondent's memory may be poor, incomplete or faulty
- It is not always easy to set up interview sessions

Observation

- Used when non-numerical data is required.
- The researcher records observations according to a predetermined schedule.
- The researcher must have a set of criteria so he/she knows what he/she is looking for.

Strengths

- Yield in-depth information
- Allow the researcher more flexibility
- Can yield a lot of data
- Less affected by respondents' biases and possible interference

Weaknesses

- Time-consuming
- Samples are often quite small
- Can yield a lot of irrelevant data
- Can be affected by the researcher's biases
- Reactions of the respondents may be misinterpreted
- Important and relevant data may be missed if chosen times of observation are not appropriate

Reliability and validity of data collection methods

Reliability

- This refers to how accurately and consistently the data collection methods or research instruments performed.
- A data collection method will produce reliable information if the design of the instrument is appropriate. If it is not then this could affect reliability as the data collected may be irrelevant and useless.
- Information can be said to be reliable if the methods used procure the same data every time, under the same conditions. The research must be replicable.

Validity

- Validity, to the researcher, refers to the extent to which the data collection methods or the research instruments, such as the questionnaire, interview and observation, actually measure what they are supposed to measure.
- Data collection involves taking samples. If the research has validity, the sample is a true representation of the population under consideration and the results of the research can be generalised.

Evaluating information

This section will remind you how to evaluate the effect of primary and secondary sources, context and medium (or channel) on the reliability and validity of information.

Primary sources

- A primary source provides original data (information) or facts on the topic under study.
- If a document was created during the actual time under study and provides an inside view of the topic, then this document is considered a primary source.
- Primary sources include artefacts, newspaper reports, recordings, case files, journals and logs, individuals directly connected to the topic, the Statistics Department.

Secondary sources

- A secondary source is an interpretation or analysis of original documents, events or data done at a later date. It generally presents a commentary or analysis of primary sources by someone without firsthand experience.
- Secondary sources include editorials, review articles, encyclopaedias.

To illustrate the difference between a primary and a secondary source consider these examples of sources relating to the attack on the World Trade Center, New York, on 11 September 2001.

- An objective newspaper report written by a journalist at the scene of the event on 11 September is a primary source.
- An editorial written in the same newspaper is a secondary source. The editor will not have been at the scene and is writing an opinion piece.
- Similarly, a book about terrorism is a secondary source. It is written after the event and is a synthesis of information from many sources.

Reliability and validity of information

What influence does a primary source have on the level of reliability of information received? Is this primary source valid? To what extent? Why or why not? What of the context – the situation surrounding the collection of data? Could this affect the reliability and validity of the information? What medium was used? Can it be trusted not to compromise the reliability or validity of the information?

These are questions which need to be considered when evaluating the effect of the different elements on reliability and validity. But, what is reliability? What is validity?

Reliability

- Reliability speaks to consistency, trustworthiness and dependability.
- You need to be able to look at different elements of the information – the source, the context, etc. – and say what makes this reliable. Ask yourself 'Can I trust the information I will receive from this source? Can I depend on it to be the truth?'

Exam Tip

Always remember that in evaluating information the two key elements to consider are reliability and validity. For a data source to be credible high levels of reliability and validity are the aim. Both elements are important.

Validity of information and arguments

- Logical in sequence and relevant – premise should lead logically to conclusion and both should relate to the same concept
- No mixture of fact and opinion
- Sufficient and complete
- Factually accurate
- Consistent and in agreement with what is generally known about the subject matter
- No shifts in the meaning of key terms and concepts

Validity

- Validity speaks to the cogency of the information.
- Ask yourself, 'Is the information based on sound reasoning? Does it have a logical structure? Is it supported by evidence? Can the information be considered to be incontestable?'

Always remember that in evaluating sources the two key elements to consider are reliability and validity. For a data source to be credible, high levels of reliability and validity are the aim. Both elements are important.

Reliability of sources and information

The question you need to ask is 'Can the source be trusted to provide accurate information?' A major concern is therefore authority.

There are several aspects you can look at to evaluate reliability of sources and information.

- **Author**
  Is the author an expert in the field? What qualifications does he/she have?

  For example, an article on a website about HIV written by a medical doctor has more authority than one written by someone without medical qualifications.

- **Professional standards**
  Does the author have certain professional standards? The example of a doctor immediately comes to mind.

  Similarly, academic authors who are published in academic journals or books have to conform to standards. Articles published in academic journals are peer-reviewed (checked by other academics).

  Many newspapers, especially large international ones such as *The New York Times* or *The Guardian* (UK), expect their journalists to operate within a professional approach.

- **Publisher**
  Is the publisher reputable?

  Academic publishers need to maintain their reputation for accurate factual information, so they have editors to ensure a high standard and articles are peer-reviewed.

  Publishers of newspapers and magazines need to avoid legal action for libel (telling lies about someone) so should be careful to print the truth.

- **Organisation or institution**
  If the data is from an organisation or institution, we need to evaluate their reputation and their role or responsibilities.

  For example, statistics on the economy from the Eastern Caribbean Central Bank would be considered to be highly reliable as the bank conducts the very important business of issuing banknotes and controlling the money supply in the region.

- **Research method**
  Does the research method chosen generate the necessary data?

  For example, in researching teen pregnancy would carrying out an interview of an expert generate the data needed or would a questionnaire administered to teens be a better choice?

Validity of sources and information

The question you need to ask is 'Is the data based on sound reasoning?'

A source could have a high level of reliability, for example, an academic research paper published in an academic journal by the leading expert in the field, but the data may have a low level of validity in that it might be very out of date.

Equally, it may be possible that a source might not be considered highly reliable, for example, an article on an Internet site which does not have the name of the author or organisation that maintains the site, but the data may still be valid.

In evaluating validity we need to look at accuracy and bias.

Accuracy

There are several aspects you can look at to evaluate accuracy of sources and information.

- **Currency**

  When was the data published or gathered? Could the information be out of date?

  For example, statistics on rates of HIV+ infection will need to be up-to-date to be accurate.

- **Relevance**

  Does the information relate to the circumstances you are applying it to?

  For example, will research carried out in the United States apply to the Caribbean?

- **Data collection**

  Was the data collected by reliable methods? Was it accurately recorded?

- **Sample size**

  Was the sample size large enough for generalisation to be accurate?

  With any social research, the sample size is vital in judging whether the data is representative of the population as a whole.

  For example, if a journalist of a newspaper article has only interviewed one person in a large crowd, will all points of view be represented?

- **Replicable**

  Do other sources have similar information? Would another similar piece of research have the same result? One way to assess this is to look at the references in the source.

Bias

There are several aspects you can look at to evaluate bias of sources and information.

- **Representation**

  Does the sample include all the variables within the population, such as age, gender, social class, religion, education level, which might affect response?

  Are the proportions in the sample the same as the proportions in the population?

  Even with a large sample, if the sample is not representative then bias in the data will occur.

- **Cultural bias**
  Has the data been collected by someone of the same or a different culture?

  For example, a Western researcher may misinterpret a non-Western culture and be biased due to racism, lack of understanding or other factors.

  Similarly, when researching within one's own culture, being subject to the same values and beliefs as the subjects may cause one not to question certain responses.

- **Political bias**
  Is the data being presented from either a right-wing or a left-wing perspective?

  The conservative agenda (e.g. free market economics, personal liberty above all other rights, and fundamentalist views) will differ from the liberal agenda (e.g. some control of the market for social gain, social control for the good of society, religious tolerance).

- **Social bias**
  Aspects such as gender, race, age and social class may affect the presentation of data.

  For example, a woman's perspective on sexual equality may differ from a man's.

- **Faulty research methods**
  Even the best academic researchers can make mistakes and inexperienced researchers, such as students, may have issues with poorly designed and executed questionnaires and interviews.

  Mistakes within the research method inadvertently cause bias. This is why academic research is reviewed by several other academics to evaluate the methodology and avoid bias in the conclusions or faulty conclusions.

- **Aim of the source in presenting the data**
  The reason for the data being presented may cause bias.

  For example, a government might present certain statistics on economic performance if they are favourable, and might avoid others. Whilst the data is valid, there might still be bias in that other relevant information is not present.

  If the source's aim is persuasive, again there may be bias. For example, commercial sites wishing to sell products.

The Internet as a source

The Internet is a source of information in the same way as a library is. You can find a huge range of both primary and secondary data through its various platforms:

- newspaper websites;
- university websites;
- journals and periodicals;
- social media websites;
- blogs;
- encyclopaedias;
- commercial sites.

The difference is that anybody can publish anything on the Internet.

Advantages of the Internet as a source

- Provides data that may sometimes be difficult to access by other means.
- Provides a wide variety of data.
- Allows researchers to compare and contrast data.
- Allows researchers to engage in more comprehensive research.
- Carries up-to-date information.
- Less time-consuming than using other sources of information.
- Less expensive than using other sources of information.

For example, an author may publish an academic paper on the Internet. That same paper may have been rejected by an academic journal.

It is therefore very important to check the reliability and validity of Internet sources and information.

- Check the author's credentials to determine the authority and reliability of the information presented.
- Check that the source is reputable; addresses ending .gov and .edu tend to be good sources.
- Ensure there is an author sponsor.
- Is there any contact information given?
- Is there any reason for author biases?
- Check for a copyright symbol on the page.
- Ensure the website is kept up-to-date and is being maintained.
- Always verify the information you find on a website by looking at other sites to see if the information is consistent with the general consensus.

The extract for items 1–7 is available as an audio track at https://www.collins.co.uk/page/Caribbean. (Alternatively, you can read it on page 154.)

<u>Items 1–7</u>

<u>Instructions</u>: **You will hear an extract. It will be read twice. Listen carefully before answering the questions based on the extract.**

1. What is the MAIN idea in the extract?
   A. When a king dies no one cares about his property.
   B. When someone dies his property, without a caretaker, falls into disrepair.
   C. If you squat on a piece of land, you will be evicted and have to leave everything.
   D. The person lived like a king but had to leave his property when things got bad.

2. What details support the main idea of the extract?
   I. 'trees, wild birds troubled the window'
   II. 'spiders locked the door'
   III. 'senatorial lizards inhabited his chair'
   A. I and II only
   B. I and III only
   C. II and III only
   D. I, II and III

3. Which of the following BEST reflects the author's purpose in the first stanza?
   A. To show that a king can live on a hill.
   B. To paint a picture of the condition of the hill when the person was alive.
   C. To show the simplicity and dignity with which the person was living.
   D. To compare the life of a king to the life of the person on a hill.

4. All the following are examples of personification except
   A. 'uncivil wind'
   B. 'wind snarled anarchy'
   C. 'spiders locked the door'
   D. 'senatorial lizards'

5. Identify the literary device used in: 'The parliament of dreams / dissolved. The shadows tilted where leaf-white, senatorial lizards / inhabited his chair'.
   A. Juxtaposition
   B. Pathetic fallacy
   C. Irony
   D. Extended metaphor

6. Based on the poem, 'after his deposition' most likely means
   A. a period following the person's confession.
   B. the time after the person's death.
   C. a period after the person has been evicted.
   D. a time after the person has abandoned the place.

7. Which of the following comments BEST highlights the effectiveness of the phrase 'spiders locked the door, / threading the shuddered moths, / and stabbed their twilight needles through / that grey republic'?
   A. The phrase emphasises how unkempt the place had become since the person's deposition.
   B. The phrase helps us to visualise the spiders as the new tenants and how they kept the place.
   C. The phrase reflects how the spiders' webs spread and caught moths in the doorway.
   D. The phrase creates an image of the spiders locking the doors and barricading the kingdom with the web.

The extract for items 8–14 is available as an audio track at https://www.collins.co.uk/page/Caribbean. (Alternatively, you can read it on page 155.)

Items 8–14

Instructions: You will hear an extract. It will be read twice. Listen carefully before answering the questions based on the extract.

8. What is the MAIN idea in the extract?

    A. Tourism has both positive and negative effects on the Caribbean.

    B. The island is no longer beautiful because of tourism.

    C. The island has exchanged its culture and freedom for tourism development.

    D. Tourism has taken over and destroyed the culture of a small and rural community.

9. Which of the following does NOT support the main idea of the extract?

    A. 'first free port to die of tourism'

    B. 'blighted with sun'

    C. 'only the crime rate is on the rise'

    D. 'our new Empire's civilized exchange / … for the good life'

10. The phrase 'sun-stoned Frederiksted' is an example of

    A. personification.

    B. metaphor.

    C. assonance.

    D. oxymoron.

11. The expression 'A condominium drowns / in vacancy' suggests that

    A. all the tourists have gone and so the condominiums flood when it rains because they are vacant.

    B. the condominiums are empty and quiet.

    C. all the rooms in the condominiums are available for rental.

    D. no tourists are coming to the island so the condominiums are unoccupied and business is dying.

12. Which of the following best describes the tone of the poet?

    A. Sarcastic and disapproving.

    B. Restrained and admiring.

    C. Controlled and cynical.

    D. Cynical and bitter.

13. According to the poem, 'the crime rate is on the rise'. Why?

    A. Tourism has caused price reduction and economic stagnation so some islanders have turned to crime.

    B. The islanders are trying to drive away the tourists with crime.

    C. The increase in tourism introduces a lot of criminal activities.

    D. Things are cheaper because of tourism so the islanders are robbing the business places.

14. Which of the following is the MOST appropriate comment on the effectiveness of the phrase 'only a jeweled housefly drones / over the bargains. The roulettes spin / rustily to the wind'?

    A. The phrase shows the activities of the tourists admiring the bargains and gambling in the casinos.

    B. The phrase helps the audience to appreciate the various sounds and sights created by tourist activities.

    C. The phrase creates a picture for the audience of what is taking place on the island.

    D. The phrase helps the audience to visualise the abject emptiness, desertion and ruin of the island.

Items 15–17

Instructions: Read the following scenario carefully and then answer items 15–17.

Professor Barrett is a linguist who does research on ancient languages. She wants to conduct research on Tapamakon, a language that is fast becoming extinct, with only two surviving original speakers – one 89 and the other 101 – and a small number of neighbouring villagers who know some amount of Tapamakon.

15. Which of the following is the most suitable source for gathering data?

    A. A 15-year-old case study on Tapamakon.

    B. The great-grand-children of the two surviving speakers.

    C. A website about archaic languages.

    D. The two surviving speakers of Tapamakon.

16. Which of the following are benefits you could outline to Professor Barrett of using interviews as her main data collection method?

    A. Less time-consuming than other methods.

    B. Comparatively lessens respondents' bias and possible interference.

    C. Provides in-depth information and opportunity for clarification.

    D. Facilitates data collection of a large population.

17. Which of the following would Professor Barrett need to do in order to conduct her research?

    A. Choose a sample that is representative of the population that speaks Tapamakon.

    B. Review articles and case studies to get background information on Tapamakon.

    C. Interview the original speakers but not the others.

    D. Draft her interview schedule and seek permission from the Tapamakon speakers.

Items 18–20

<u>Instructions</u>: **Read the following scenario carefully and then answer items 18–20.**

Kenton is doing his Communications IA on the topic: 'The CCJ – Promoting Effective Jurisprudence in Jamaica'. He has found a *Gleaner* article that he thinks may be helpful. His teacher has asked him to evaluate the article.

   This is the article.

Show Pride And Go With CCJ – Government Senator

A long-standing Government senator said yesterday that Jamaicans would be lacking in pride if they dare to hang on to the Judicial Committee of the Privy Council as the country's final court of appeal.

Navel Clarke, a trade unionist by profession, said in the Senate yesterday that 'we must show our pride' and move away from the Privy Council and embrace the Caribbean Court of Justice (CCJ) in its appellate jurisdiction.

'They are begging us, they are pushing us, they have said things that I don't think anybody with any pride would want to continue to endure,' said Clarke, who has also lived in England.

The Government senator was making his contribution to the debate on three CCJ bills that are now before the Senate.

The debate had been suspended due to a boycott of the Senate by opposition members but two of the eight, Tom Tavares-Finson and Kavan Gayle, showed up yesterday.

Clarke, noting that former Prime Minister Hugh Shearer in 1970 proposed that Jamaica join with other regional countries to form a Caribbean Court, said that for the Opposition members to now turn its back on an idea cultivated by one of their leaders defies logic.

By: Daraine Luton (Senior Staff Reporter)

The Gleaner, November 6, 2015

---

18. Which of the following aspects of the data source can help Kenton to determine the reliability of the data it provides?

  I.   Author

  II. Publisher

  III. Date of publication

  A. I and II only

  B. I and III only

  C. II and III only

  D. I, II and III

19. The article may be subjective because

  A. it contains cultural biases.

  B. it contains political biases.

  C. the research methods are flawed.

  D. the aim of the source is biased.

20. Two arguments for reliability and validity are:

  A. the article is referenced and in a reputable paper.

  B. the article was published by *The Gleaner* and speaks about parliament.

  C. the article was recently published in a reputable paper and written by an expert journalist.

  D. the article has information that can be found in other sources and the publishing company is well known.

Items 21–23

<u>Instructions</u>: **Read the following scenario carefully and then answer items 21–23.**

Kenton and Kenya are in the same 12th-grade class. Their IA topics are similar so they decide to team up to collect data and review sources. However, they have very different ideas on how to go about evaluating the sources and what data-gathering instruments to use, as well as who their sample will be. Ms Kentish, their Communication Studies teacher, gave them some guidelines and criteria for evaluation.

21. Validity of information is determined if the argument is

    I.   based on good judgement, reasoning and evidence.

    II.   sound, logical, incontestable.

    III.   contains factually accurate statements.

    A. I and II only

    B. I and III only

    C. II and III only

    D. I, II and III

22. Ms Kentish would likely have said: 'When your research instruments perform accurately and consistently, you can say your data is

    A. credible.'

    B. reliable.'

    C. valid.'

    D. authentic.'

23. Which of the following is unlikely to have been listed by Ms Kentish as a factor to consider in determining a sample?

    A. It must be randomly selected.

    B. It must be sufficient and adequate.

    C. It must be representative.

    D. It must contain all the variables present within the population.

Chapter 3

Module 2: Language and Community

Objectives

This chapter will help you revise these objectives:

- discuss the concept of language;
- identify the salient features of one Creole or Creole-influenced vernacular (in your territory or any other territory) which make it different from Caribbean Standard English;
- explain the challenges faced by the Creole or the Creole-influenced vernacular speaker in learning Caribbean Standard English;
- evaluate the role of language in Caribbean identity;
- analyse the social, political, ethical and psychological roles of language in human societies;
- describe your territory or any other territory along the following lines:
  - the range of languages (including Creoles);
  - the influence of history on the language situation;
  - attitudes to languages used;
  - the potential of these attitudes for integration, marginalisation and alienation;
- assess the use of registers, dialects, ranges of formality and other aspects of language in various types of interactive settings;
- identify the technological advances that have impacted on communication;
- examine how communication is affected and effected by the use of technology in different cultural settings and interactive contexts.

Introduction

In Module 2 the emphasis is on understanding language, the cultural norms within the Caribbean region, how language is used and what influences can change a language. Given the individual characteristics of each Caribbean country, there will be distinct variations in the way words sound and are spelt due to the history and influences experienced by each country. You will need to know what language is, its function and characteristics, as well as know the history of Creole languages and the differences between Standard Caribbean English and Creole.

Language

This section will remind you how to discuss the concept of language.

When we think of language we need to make a distinction between the general concept of language and the specific concept of a language.

- Language is the ability of humans to express themselves through words that define our inner feelings, describe what we see or hear, explain how we understand the world around us and express our thoughts. It is a characteristic that separates humans from the rest of the animal kingdom.
- A language is any distinct system of verbal expression. This means that a language is distinguishable from other languages because of certain characteristics, namely structure and vocabulary.

So, English, Spanish, Jamaican and Portuguese are examples of different languages and in expressing themselves verbally, the speakers of these languages are using language.

Functions of language

We use language every day for a variety of purposes. When we apologise for inappropriate actions, ask permission or express our desires we are using language to fulfil these purposes.

Language is both external (in the form of sounds and symbols) and internal (in the form of mental activity – thinking and remembering).

Humans use language in order to:

- communicate
  - have simple or complex conversations
  - comprehend new and unfamiliar ideas
  - rearrange and communicate thoughts in new and different ways
  - create an infinite number of new utterances and understand ones never heard before
- persuade (cognitive)
- question
- direct (through commands and requests)
  - to cause or prevent overt action

- provide aesthetic pleasure
  - through the creation of literary work
  - by evoking and expressing certain feelings
- inform
  - by describing the world or reasoning about it
  - by affirming or denying propositions
  - by expressing truth values
- reflect
  - to process and use past experiences
  - allows for human invention
- provide and/or reinforce a sense of identity
  - form bonds with other users of a language
  - each user has their own idiolect which marks them off as different from others
- create and enforce rules
- perform rituals (ceremonial function)

  Examples: 'Dearly beloved, we are gathered here today to join this couple in holy matrimony …'; 'Ashes to ashes, dust to dust …'

Characteristics of language

- **Human trait**
  Although other species of animals have systems of communication that allow them to perform basic functions (some species can even learn words), they are unable to respond in a full sentence, articulate an emotional response or conduct conversations with the range and complexity with which human beings do.

- **Naturally acquired**
  Humans acquire and learn language as part of our normal development; we learn to speak our mother tongue without structured lessons.

  Babies babble as they imitate the words used by the adults around them until eventually they start to form words and then construct simple sentences.

- **Maturational**
  As people age, their ability to understand and use language increases. Adults tend to be able to construct more complex sentences than children and have a greater vocabulary.

- **Verbal**
  Language is first spoken and then written.

- **Systematic**
  There is order in how sound patterns are pronounced and how words are used. Language is rule-governed.

- **Symbolic**
  A word is a symbol representing something: a person, a feeling, an action, an abstract idea. There are nouns and verbs but also adjectives, adverbs, conjunctions and other types of word. Language gives meaning to these symbols.

  For example, English speakers know what the words 'thank you' mean. In French, the same meaning is attached to a different symbol, 'merci'.

Note

Ten years ago finding information for a research project involved a trip to the library and perhaps a webpage. Today the term 'google' is universally accepted as a word meaning 'look it up on the Internet'. A new word has entered the English vocabulary because new technology exists. However, there is another aspect to this change. 'Google' is the name of a search engine and as such is a noun. The use of nouns as verbs has become more common in recent years, particularly in connection with technology.

This is one example of how a language has changed in response to new technology.

Make a note of other changes in language resulting from other influences.

Note

In some Caribbean countries the range of languages spoken is said to occur on a continuum, with basilect at the lower end, acrolect at the higher end and mesolect in the middle. They are not described as language varieties. Speakers using the basilect would be speaking Creole; those using the acrolect would be speaking Caribbean Standard English and those using the mesolect would be using a mixture of the two. Speakers can communicate at different points on the continuum depending on the situation.

- **Dynamic**
  Language is always changing all the time.
  The meanings of words can change over time.
  New words can appear and be accepted by the masses without discussion.
  Some words fall out of use.
  Language evolves in response to changes and differences in the societies and communities using it.
  Factors which can cause change in a language include:
- education;
- class;
- age;
- migration;
- popular culture;
- commerce;
- technology.

Exam Tip

Paper 2 exam questions are often based on texts that are in both Creole and Caribbean Standard English.

You may be asked to explain and discuss how or why people use language varieties, dialects and accents. Each serves a distinct function and you will need to know and understand how they are used and why.

Language varieties, dialects and accents

What is a language variety?

A language variety is, simply put, a form of a language. It may be a dialect, a standard language, a register or another form of a language.

Language variation is speakers' ability to use the different forms of language to suit their communication needs depending on the context they are in, for example whether they are in a social setting or the work place, whether they are communicating with their peers or in communication with somebody from a different level in a hierarchical situation.

In the Caribbean, language variations are based on Caribbean Standard English and Creole. Variation also includes the use of particular styles or different levels of formality.

Useful terms

- **Vernacular**
  The commonly spoken language or dialect of a particular people or place.

- **Standard language**
  The language or dialect of a country used for formal and official purposes, such as education.

- **Creole**
  A language formed when there is contact between people who speak different languages.
  It is based on a combination of features of the original languages, along with its own new features.

Caribbean English Creoles tend to have vocabulary based on English but grammar that shares many features with West African languages.

- **Accent**
  This refers to how words sound.

  Different accents across the Caribbean result in the same word sounding different when spoken by people from different countries, regions or social backgrounds.

  For example, the word written as 'mother' in Caribbean Standard English might be pronounced 'mother', 'mudder' or 'mooder' depending on where the speaker comes from.

- **Dialect**
  A variety of a language spoken by a particular social, geographical or cultural group of people.

  Dialects tend to differ in vocabulary and pronunciation rather than in grammar.

  A dialect is not 'bad' English. Caribbean Standard English, British Standard English and American Standard English are all dialects of English. There are also non-standard dialects, such as Black English/ Ebonics in the USA and Cockney in England.

- **Register**
  A style of speaking or writing used in particular situations, ranging from very formal to very informal.

- **Code switch**
  Using more than one language variety during a conversation or even within a sentence.

Creole and Creole-influenced vernacular

This section will remind you how to:

- identify the salient features of one Creole or Creole-influenced vernacular which make it different from Caribbean Standard English;
- explain the challenges faced by the Creole or the Creole-influenced vernacular speaker in learning Caribbean Standard English.

Features of Creole languages

There are several features of Creole and Creole-influenced vernacular which make them different from Caribbean Standard English. They include:

- grammar (syntax);
- sound (phonology);
- vocabulary (lexicon – words, and semantics – meanings).

Note that, because English Creole spelling systems are still emerging, spelling of Creole words varies.

Remember

One of the characteristics of language is that it is systematic or rule-governed.

Activity

Listen to or read the works of Caribbean writers and poets such as Louise Bennett-Coverley, Joanne C. Hillhouse, Olive Senior and Kwame Dawes and compare how they use Caribbean Standard English and Creole, and note the cultural differences.

Grammar

Grammar is part of the system of rules that govern a language.

Creole languages are governed by a different systems of rules from Caribbean Standard English.

These are realised in the different characteristics of grammar outlined in your syllabus and reviewed below.

Useful terms

- **Copula**

    A copula links the subject to the predicate (i.e. the part of the sentence which is saying something about the subject). It is verb, often the verb 'be'. It can also be called a linking verb.

- **Morpheme**

    A morpheme is a word or part of a word that serves a grammatical function.

- **Marked vs unmarked**

    Marked vs unmarked refers to the presence or absence of a morpheme.

    For example:

    In Caribbean Standard English, the morpheme 's' is used to signal the grammatical function of pluralisation (more than one) as in 'books' so 'book' is marked.

    In English Creole, 'book' can also be marked for pluralisation but with morpheme 'dem', which follows the noun, as in 'book dem'.

    When a word is unmarked for pluralisation it means the plural marker is absent, which is sometimes the case in English Creole.

Characteristics of grammar

English Creole (EC)	Caribbean Standard English (CSE)
When count nouns are used inclusively or collectively (that is in reference to all things that fall in that category) they are unmarked for pluralisation.	Caribbean Standard English pluralises count nouns with generic meaning.
Example: '**Bwai** wear khaki.'	Example: '**Boys** wear khaki.'
Action verbs that are used to refer to past activity are unmarked.	Action verbs with past time reference are marked for past tense.
Example: 'Mi **it** di food we did ina di fridge.'	Example: 'I **ate** the food that was in the fridge.'
EC uses preverbal markers (markers that precede the verb) to indicate tense: **behn/bin/wehn/did** (past marker) **go** (future marker) **a** (marker of continuous and habitual) **does** (marker of habitual) Examples: 'Mi wehn gaa school.' 'Im go do it.' 'Mi mada a wash.' 'You does say so every time.' NB: Verbs are unmarked for agreement with a singular noun. Example: 'Kam **eat** wid a fork.' This structure therefore resembles the CSE structure when the sentence has a plural noun. Example: 'Kam and Naila **eat** with a fork.'	CSE uses auxiliaries and suffixes to mark verbs for tense: **did/-ed** (past) **will/shall** (future) **-ing** (continuous) simple present tense forms (cook, cooks) Examples: 'I went to school.' 'He will do it.' 'My mother is washing.' 'You always say that.' Verbs are marked with an 's' for agreement with singular nouns. Example: 'Kam **eats** with a fork.'

English Creole (EC)	Caribbean Standard English (CSE)
EC tends to have zero-copula constructions. EC uses subject–adjective structures instead. Examples: 'Naila kind.' 'Mi hungry.' Other examples of zero-copula structures: 'Mi mada de home.' 'Yu behaving bad.' Note: You could also say EC tends not to use auxiliary verbs.	CSE uses subject–copula–adjective structures. Examples: 'Naila **is** kind.' 'I **am** hungry.' 'My mother **is** at home.' 'You **are** behaving badly'.
In question formation, EC uses subject–verb word order (the subject comes before the verb), along with a rising intonation. Example: '**Yu done do** yu homework?'	CSE uses subject–auxiliary inversion (the positions subject and auxiliary are reversed so the auxiliary comes before the subject) in question formation, together with rising intonation. Example: '**Have you finished** your homework?'
Pluralisation is signalled by the addition of 'dem' after the noun. Examples: 'Di man **dem**' 'Di two book **dem**' (emphasising the numerical marker)	CSE uses the plural marker 's' or changes the word internally as seen in the examples below. Examples: 'The men' 'The two book**s**'
EC uses front-focusing to highlight certain elements within a sentence. Examples: 'Is **Susan** eat di chicken?' (focuses on who did the eating) 'Is **di chicken** Susan eat?' (focuses on what was eaten)	CSE often uses pronunciation by verbally stressing that which is to be emphasised. Examples: '**Susan** ate the chicken?' (The word 'Susan' is stressed to focus on who did the eating.) 'Susan ate **the chicken**?' (The words 'the chicken' are stressed to focus on what was eaten.)
EC uses the morpheme 'fi' to indicate ownership (possession). Example: 'A **fi** Kaydene handout.'	CSE uses an apostrophe + 's' ('s) as the possessive marker. It is attached to the noun to indicate possession. Example: 'It is Kaydene**'s** handout.'
EC uses 'ain' or 'aint'; 'nehn' or 'nay' and 'noh' as negators. Examples: 'De **aint** gat none.' 'I **aint** goin to di party tonight.' 'Mi **nehn** go.' 'Sim **nehn** se so.' 'Mi **noh** know.'	CSE uses 'didn't', 'don't', 'not' and 'never' as negators. Examples: 'They **don't** have any.' 'I am **not** going to the party tonight.' 'I **didn't** go.' 'Sim **never** said that.' 'I **don't** know.'
Some words have different functions based on where they are used in the sentence. Example: '**Wi** a gaa maakit.' ('Wi' is used as a personal pronoun when in this position.) 'Yu know is fi **wi** language.' ('wi' is used as a possessive pronoun when in this position.)	CSE does not change the function of words in this way. Example: '**We** are going to the market.' 'You know that it is **our** language.'
EC allows a double negative (i.e. two negatives) in its sentence construction. Examples: 'Mi **don't** want **none**.' 'Ricky **naa** talk to **nobody**.'	A double negative in CSE is generally considered an error of grammar. CSE use 'any' or a word with 'any' as a part of its construction. Examples: 'I **don't** want **any**.' 'Ricky is **not** talking to **any**body.'

This is the sound system of a language.

English Creole has a sound system independent of Caribbean Standard English. This means that the pronunciations of English Creole words are not influenced by Caribbean Standard English. The phonological characteristics are important in distinguishing English Creole from what may be considered Caribbean Standard English.

Useful terms

- **Consonant clusters**

    A group of consonants which have no intervening vowel.
    Example: 'sch' and 'ls' in 'schools' are consonant clusters.

- **Voiced vs voiceless**

    Consonant sounds may be voiced or voiceless.

    When a consonant sound is voiced, there is a vibration that accompanies its pronunciation as in that which is felt when you pronounce the /z/ sound in 'zero'.

    When a consonant sound is voiceless, there is no such vibration, for example, when you pronounce the /s/ sound in 'sound'.

    You can test whether a sound is voiced or voiceless by placing your fingers on your voice box when you pronounce the sound.

Characteristics of phonology

English Creole (EC)	Caribbean Standard English (CSE)
EC tends to avoid consonant clusters at the end of words, whether voiced or voiceless; so in many cases the final sound is omitted. This is called segment reduction – the cluster is considered to be a segment.	Both voiced and voiceless consonant clusters at the end of words are maintained.
Examples: Words ending with: [nd] → [n] – 'tan', 'ban' [st] and [sed] → [s] – 'firs', 'bless' [ft] and [ghed] → [f] – 'lif', 'cough' [ped] → [p] – 'gulp', 'reap'	Examples: Words ending with: [nd] – 'stand', 'band' [st] and [sed] – 'first', 'blessed' [ft] and [ghed] – 'lift', 'coughed' [ped] – 'gulped', 'reaped'
EC does not use the [th] sound. It substitutes a [t] sound for the voiceless [th] sound and [d] for the voiced [th] sound at the beginning and end of a word or syllable. When an /f/ sound precedes the [th], the [th] sound is omitted altogether.	CSE uses both the voiceless and the voiced [th] sound.
Examples: Voiceless Voiced 'team' 'di' 'tik' 'dese' 'etics' 'rada' 'atlete' 'eida' 'maratan' 'bood' 'girt' 'breed' 'trut' 'fif' and 'twelv(f)'	Examples: Voiceless Voiced 'theme' 'the' 'thick' 'these' 'ethics' 'rather' 'athlete' 'either' 'marathon' 'booth' 'girth' 'breathe' 'truth' 'fifth' and 'twelfth'

English Creole (EC)	Caribbean Standard English (CSE)
There are some words whose pronunciations are altered in EC because the sounds are rearranged or even changed. This is called metathesis.	No metathesis in CSE.
Examples: 'aks', 'deks' 'cerfiticate' 'interduce' 'iern' 'flim' 'voilence'	Examples: 'ask', 'desk' 'certificate' 'introduce' 'iron' 'film' 'violence'
Another phonological characteristic that sometimes occurs in EC is that in words where the sound /t/ is followed by /l/, the pronunciation changes from /tl/ to /kl/ and where there is /dl/ it changes to /gl/	
Examples: 'bokl' 'kekl' 'cangl' 'neegl'	Examples: 'bottle' 'kettle' 'candle' 'needle'
EC pronouns have shorter vowel sounds than CSE.	Vowel sounds are longer in CSE.
Examples: 'shi' 'wi' 'mi' 'yu'	Examples: 'she' 'we' 'me' 'you'

Vocabulary

When we talk about vocabulary we are looking at the words (lexical items) in the language and the meanings (semantics) associated with these words. Although the lexical items are English-based, many of the words have different meanings in Creole and are used in non-English ways.

Characteristics of vocabulary

English Creole (EC)	Caribbean Standard English (CSE)
EC and CSE share words but the words have different meanings.	
Examples: ignorant = easily angered dark = not very exposed; not sensible belly = pregnant craven = greedy	Examples: ignorant = lacking in knowledge dark = little or no light; colour or shade belly = stomach craven = cowardly
EC has some peculiar lexical items and phrases; some are adopted from other non-English languages.	
Examples: pikini/pikni unu/allyuh carry-go-bring-come tan-todi mout-a-massi out-a-order wanga-gut all a unu/all a wunna	Equivalents: small child plural you rumour-monger be still, stop talkative rude, ill-mannered greedy everyone

Activities

1. Make a list of vocabulary in Creole languages from across the region and the equivalents in Caribbean Standard English.
    Test your friends to see if they can identify country of origin.
2. Make a list of examples from your own country.
3. Watch local news programmes and note the words used by witnesses to an incident and compare them with those used in the newsreader's summary of the story.

English Creole (EC)	Caribbean Standard English (CSE)
EC and CSE share words but the words are different parts of speech.	
Examples: tief = n, v deaf = v, adj dung = prep	Examples: thief = n deaf = adj dung = n, v
Some CSE words are compounded to create nouns in EC that are not present in CSE.	
Examples: foot bottom eye water age paper badwud	Equivalents: sole of the foot tears birth certificate profanity/expletive
Some EC words are created by reduplicating all or part of CSE words.	
Examples: friedi friedi = fearful/timid chati chati = talk excessively or out of turn foo fool = stupid back back = reverse	CSE base: afraid chatty foolish backwards
There are also some EC lexical items that seem to take their origins from CSE words, they share similar meanings to the CSE words, but their pronunciation is different.	
Examples: gravalicious (adj) = greedy cumoojin (adj) = weird or miserly (depending on the particular variety of Creole) cubbitch = (v, adj) to begrudge, mean	Examples: avaricious (adj) = greedy curmudgeon (n) = bad tempered or mean person covetous (adj) = wanting to possess something
EC uses onomatopoeic words as adverbs.	
Examples: splat – 'Shi drop **splat** a grung.' braps – 'The way Peter frighten, him stop **braps**, same time.' buff – 'Shi run an go **buff** ina di wall.'	

These examples are obviously not exhaustive. Use them to guide your general revision. Remember that the exam is set not just for your country or territory but for the whole region.

You need to identify the features that are non-standard and use your knowledge of grammar, phonology and vocabulary to discuss what makes them different from the standard form.

Challenges faced by the Creole speaker in learning Caribbean Standard English

Technical challenges

Many of the challenges faced by the Creole speaker in learning Caribbean Standard English are those faced by anybody learning a different language. They stem from the differences between the language learner's own language and the language he/she is learning. However, because of the similarities between English Creole and Caribbean Standard English, it is necessary to master the differences in order for it to be recognised that Caribbean Standard English is being used.

The challenges are compounded for the Creole speaker because both languages are encountered in everyday life and because speakers may switch between them depending on the situation.

Exam Tip

In order to identify the technical challenges faced by the Creole speaker in learning Caribbean Standard English, you need to be familiar with the features that make English Creole different from Caribbean Standard English discussed in the previous section.

- **Grammar**
Different grammatical rules govern sentence structure, tense marking and usage in English Creole and Caribbean Standard English. If Creole speakers are not aware of the rules, it will be difficult for them to separate the two languages.

  Also, because Creole speakers have a wide variety of ways to express thoughts, they may have difficulty understanding or using the rules of Caribbean Standard English.

- **Phonology**
Differences in how sounds are pronounced in the mother tongue and the language being learned are among the most difficult for a language learner to overcome, and indeed some of the characteristics of English Creole are carried over to Caribbean Standard English.

  However, the differences in pronunciation can distort understanding as ambiguities may occur. For example, a Creole speaker may confuse the meanings of 'heat' and 'eat'. The differences can also affect how well Creole speakers spell and recognise read Caribbean Standard English words.

  Another problem Creole speakers may have is hyper-correction. For example, because the /h/ sound at the beginning of words tends not to be pronounced in English Creole, some speakers may add an /h/ sound at the beginning of words that do not require it, usually those beginning with a vowel. For example, 'exam' may become 'hexam', 'office' may become 'hoffice'.

- **Vocabulary**
Because the lexical base of English Creole and Caribbean Standard English is the same, it is difficult for the Creole speaker to recognise and use correctly the shared words with different meanings or different parts of speech.

  In addition, there are some words and phrases in Caribbean Standard English which have a range of meanings, some of which may be quite idiomatic, which have just a literal interpretation in English Creole. For example, 'to run over'.

Socio-cultural challenges

- **Lack of reinforcement**
Having said the Creole speaker will encounter both languages, in the Caribbean English Creole is the vernacular of the majority. This means that for Creole speakers learning Caribbean Standard English, there is often not much opportunity for practice and reinforcement outside the formal educational setting, and this impedes their progress in acquiring Caribbean Standard English.

- **Educational methods**
Being taught Caribbean Standard English as though it is the first language further complicates the issue, especially when the Creole speaker is being taught that English Creole expressions present in his/ her work are errors instead of conflicting language rules.

- **The oral nature of English Creole**
Because English Creole is largely oral, many Creole speakers have no written frame of reference for writing Caribbean Standard English and the speech patterns of Creole speakers can interfere with their writing of Caribbean Standard English.

Language in society

This section will remind you how to analyse the social, political, ethical and psychological roles of language in human societies.

Language is one of the principle factors allowing humans to live together in communities. A community might be a small group, such as a friendship group at school, or might be as large as a nation or even a region.

The language, or languages, spoken by a community is one way in which it is identified.

Language can signal position in society, educational background and geographic origins, among other things. It can be used to show solidarity with others or a social distance from them. It can express identity. In the Caribbean, these functions are possible through the choice of language variety (the form of language used).

Within the Caribbean and the wider world, language is used both positively and negatively. Some of these uses are reviewed below.

- **To discriminate against others**
  Speakers of non-standard varieties may be treated unfairly because of their use of language. This could include not just using a non-standard form but also having a limited vocabulary or using the accent of a minority group.

  Speakers of non-standard varieties may be turned away at a job interview or suspected of wrongdoing for these reasons.

  They may be made to feel inferior to a speaker of the standard form, often being told to 'speak properly' or having their speech criticised.

  They may be judged as being uneducated, from the inner city, being 'country' (i.e. being from a rural area) or even being a dunce because of the language they use.

  Today Caribbean nationals are discriminated against on an international scale simply for having a Caribbean accent. This may be due to the rise in scamming perpetuated by Caribbean criminals, and results in many Caribbean nationals facing discrimination when they travel outside the Caribbean or when they attempt to conduct business internationally via the telephone.

- **To alienate**
  People can use language, both standard and non-standard forms, to make another person feel like an outsider.

  When a group of people are familiar with more than one language variety and wish to exclude another person who is not familiar with one of those language varieties, the group can use the unfamiliar language even when they might not usually use it. This happens with in-groups, peers, social groups or even with strangers in an airport departure lounge. Have you ever experienced being among people who were speaking your language who then switch to another language? Maybe going into a Chinese restaurant or an Indian-owned and operated store?

  This is done to put distance between the group and the outsider. Even Caribbean nationals do it, especially when travelling overseas and among other nationalities. They will from time to time go into their various Creole languages to discuss anything they do not want the foreigner to understand.

Members of the social elite may use the standard language to distance themselves from the hired help. Even if among their friends they usually speak at the lower end of the continuum, in the presence of the hired help, who may be a Creole speaker, they may switch to the higher end of the continuum to indicate that the hired help is not a member of their group.

Teenagers create coded language with which they communicate with each other. They will use these codes among themselves and in the company of their parents, teachers or even other teenagers who are not a part of their in-group. They often use slang and abbreviated terms that may exclude the older generation if they are not familiar with the meanings of these expressions.

- **To make face threats**
  To 'save face' is to maintain one's good reputation.

  A 'face threat' is a vocalised act that threatens someone's reputation.

  Whenever people engage in quarrels or even have conversations with another person, they engage in possible face-threatening acts. What they say may embarrass or insult the other person. It may also be a compliment to the other person but take something away from themselves.

  Examples of face threats include the derogatory and defamatory comments people often make via social media about other people or in response to a photo or a status or tweet that was posted.

  However, although face threats include anything that has the potential to make a person look bad, they are not necessarily offensive in themselves. Pointing out in the presence of other people that somebody has made an error is a face-threatening act.

- **To mark social biases**
  Language is often used to demonstrate a speaker's attitude towards particular groups or individuals because of their race, gender, religion, sexual orientation or even the language they speak. Speakers, through what they say, may display their social biases. These may be in favour of or against social groups. When speakers make comments that are prejudicial or highlight a stereotype, they are marking a social bias.

  Commentators and journalists may use language to mark social biases. For instance during election campaign periods, you may find editorials that seem to favour one party over another.

  Another example of language being used to mark a social bias is a comment made by a patron at a salon. Another patron was sitting in waiting – she was light-skinned, possibly of Indian descent. The salon attendants, all dark-skinned, possibly of African descent, were conversing in English Creole when the light-skinned patron made a comment in impeccable English Creole. The first patron's subsequent comment was 'She brown an pretty and talk so bad'. This is showing a clear social bias.

  When a speaker adjusts his/her speech to accommodate another speaker this could also be displaying a social bias. For instance a speaker who uses Caribbean Standard English with somebody who is well groomed, but switches to English Creole to address somebody who is unkempt, is demonstrating a social bias.

- **To assert authority**

Language can be a tool with which people in positions of power assert their authority. This is especially true in situations where there are two language forms, one of higher prestige than the other. Speakers in certain situations may switch to or maintain use of the language of higher prestige to show that he/she has control or is the one in charge.

It may also be demonstrated by the speaker giving orders or making suggestions that exert dominance over the listener(s). As teenagers you must have experienced adults using language to assert their authority. Principals, teachers, parents and prefects can all use what they say to show that they are in charge. They have the authority.

- **To mark identity**

Language is used to provide or reinforce an individual's sense of identity in relation to his/her membership of a particular group, particularly a nationality but also a smaller group such as a particular region of a country or a larger one such as a geographical area like the Caribbean.

Using language that is similar creates a great ethnic, regional, communal or national bond. Sharing a language helps to create a sense of identity for a country's citizens.

Additionally, language allows each individual speaker to maintain his/her own uniqueness even though he/she speaks the same language as others in his/her region, country or even community. This is because each person has his/her own idiolect – particular words and phrases that he/she often uses, idiosyncrasies of usage and pronunciation, etc. No two people speak exactly alike and this identifies each person as an individual with his/her own identity.

- **To mark solidarity**

Language can be used to show solidarity within a community.

When people speak, their words can show camaraderie, sympathy, concern and affection and this helps to create a sense of mutual support and unity among the speakers.

When somebody reminds another person that he/she is from the same place or that he/she has been through the same experiences, he/she is creating a sense of solidarity.

Additionally, groups may create their own slang, specialised jargon or ritualistic greetings. Using these are a way in which the members of the group mark their solidarity.

- **To make social linkages**

Another role that language plays in society is to make social linkages, that is to establish connections with other people.

People start and establish their various relationships through what they say.

People may engage in networking, which is a form of social connection with others who can promote their mutual interests.

People who want to be accepted into a particular group may change the way they speak so that it is similar to the group they want to enter.

- **To promote cultural awareness**

    Language helps to promote cultural awareness.

    For instance, when somebody learns a second language, he/she is open to a new culture and it creates opportunities for new experiences within that culture.

    Language creates avenues for people to learn about the beliefs, customs and practices of another culture. Literature about other cultures exists because of language and this advances people's knowledge of other cultures.

    Language is in the media which bring diverse cultures to different people. Media help to create a global community and through this cultures across the world are more accessible, which means that people are exposed to many different cultures. Through films, they learn about American and European culture. People in other countries learn about the culture of the Caribbean through the music and books that come out of the region. These are all instances of language promoting cultural awareness.

Language and Caribbean identity

This section will remind you how to evaluate the role of language in Caribbean identity.

There are many characteristics that contribute to the Caribbean identity. This identity is really just a combination of shared characteristics that are used to associate someone with being Caribbean.

As it relates to language, there are certain features of pronunciation, sentence structure and vocabulary that are peculiar to speakers who are from the Caribbean.

They have a shared history and this has resulted in a diverse culture but also a range of languages. There are several language varieties, pidgins and creoles. This situation has evolved out of the early history of the region which tells the story of contributions from different parts of the world. The languages of the Caribbean have been influenced by European colonists who spoke English, French, Spanish and Dutch, among others.

The creole languages and Caribbean Standard English distinguish and unite citizens residing in the Caribbean and people of the Caribbean diaspora. Language is a large part of being 'Caribbean', in fact Caribbean nationals who speak predominantly Standard English without a noticeable Caribbean accent are often judged as not being Caribbean.

Language therefore helps to foster the Caribbean identity in that:

- speakers form a connection;
- it sets us apart, especially when living or studying outside the region;
- it creates sense of belonging;
- it can be used to exclude non-speakers;
- cross-cultural references add pride – for example, the universal 'One Love', originally associated with the Rastafarian community;
- it is expressive – there are, for example, phrases that have no Standard English equivalent, such as 'jack!' and 'a tall a tall'.

Activity

Record and listen to a portion of a parliamentary debate and make note of the number of times a speaker uses Creole to emphasise a point.

For generations schools taught in Caribbean Standard English based on the English language as taught by colonial educators. Students were encouraged to speak 'properly' as this would indicate that they were bright and from a good social background.

In the past 50 years, there has been a mini 'revolution' with regard to how we see ourselves. Part of this is due to the political road to independence. Politicians are no longer colonials or people from certain sectors of society, the rise of the unions and union leaders has resulted in politicians who can speak to the man in the fields and also to their former colonial counterparts.

Another aspect is that musicians, writers and film-makers are celebrating Caribbean languages and some their work is reaching a global audience. For example, the dancehall genre has become mainstream despite the use of Jamaican Patois; the Jamaican novelist, Marlon James won the Man Booker Prize in 2015 for the novel, *A Brief History of Seven Killings*, which is written in American English, Caribbean Standard English and Jamaican Creole/Patois; the film *Pressure* was directed by the Trinidad-born Horace Ové and has as its central theme the experiences of West Indian migrants in London.

However, although there appears to be growing pride in Caribbean languages, it is only in recent times that creole dictionaries have been developed and that creole languages have begun to be celebrated during national events such as Independence. Haiti is the only country to have made its creole language an official language. Students in schools in Haiti are taught in Standard French and French Creole.

The language situation in the Caribbean

This section will remind you how to describe your territory or any other territory in terms of the range of languages (including creoles), the influence of history on the language situation in the Caribbean, the attitudes to languages used and the potential of these attitudes for integration, marginalisation and alienation.

Territories and their languages

Country	Official language	Mass vernacular	Other languages
Anguilla	English	English Creole	
Antigua and Barbuda	English	Local dialects (English Creole based)	
Aruba and Bonaire	Dutch	Papiamentu	English, Spanish
The Bahamas	English	English Creole	
Barbados	English	English Creole	
Belize	English	English Creole	Spanish, Mayan, Garifuna
Bermuda	English	Bermudian English	French, Spanish
British Virgin Islands	English	English	
Cuba	Spanish	Spanish	
Curaçao	Dutch	Papiamentu	French, Spanish
Dominica	English	English Creole, French Creole	
Dominican Republic	Spanish	Spanish	English, French Creole

Country	Official language	Mass vernacular	Other languages
Grenada	English	English Creole	French Creole
Guadeloupe and Martinique	French	French Creole	English
Guyana	English	English Creole	Bhojpuri Hindi, Amerindian
Haiti	French, French Creole	French Creole	
Jamaica	English	English Creole/Jamaican Patois	
Puerto Rico	Spanish	Spanish	English
St Kitts and Nevis and Montserrat	English	English Creole	
St Lucia	English	French Creole English Creole	
St Martin/St Maarten	French, Dutch	Papiamentu, English	Haitian Creole, French Creole, English Creole, Spanish
St Thomas	English	English	French Creole, Spanish
Suriname	Dutch	Sranan Tongo	Sarnami Hindustani, Javanese, Maroon languages (Saramaccan, Ndyuka/Aukan) Amerindian languages (Trio, Wayana)
St Vincent	English	English Creole	
Trinidad and Tobago	English	English Creoles	French Creole, Spanish, Bhojpuri Hindi

The influence of history

The variations of Creole spoken across the region have evolved from the influx in the 17th and 18th centuries of European colonists and enslaved people from Africa, who spoke 28 languages, and the indigenous people having to communicate with each together.

The languages that evolved were based on the dominant colonial master.

For example in Antigua, the creole language is English-based mixed with West African pidgin English and African languages such as Yoruba, Kikongo, Mandinka, Wolof, Igbo, Fante, Fon, Twi, Hausa and Bantu. However, in the French-influenced islands such as Guadeloupe and Martinique it is based on French. In the Dutch islands of Aruba, Bonaire and Curaçao the creole language is called Papiamentu (or Papiamento). It is based on Spanish and Portuguese because the original colonists were Spanish and the Dutch colonists who followed them came from Brazil and brought a Portuguese vernacular with them. It also has elements of Dutch, English, French, Arawak and African languages.

The late 19th century saw the arrival of people from the continent of India, especially to the cane-growing countries of Guyana and Trinidad and Tobago, mostly speaking Bhojpuri Hindi and some Urdu. This has added to the lexicon and speech patterns of these countries.

The late 20th century has seen the arrival of Chinese migrants as workers and also as business owners. Their impact across the region may take a few decades to notice.

Other factors affecting language

Language in the Caribbean has clearly been influenced by the history of the region. However, it has been and continues to be influenced by other factors too.

- **Social**

Language is one of the key components used in stratifying society. The language variety of the people with power becomes the standard language. Historically in the Caribbean these were the European colonists.

The standard language is seen as the language of the upper class and the educated. The prestige associated with the standard language ensures that it is one of the main vehicles of upward social mobility.

The non-standard forms are associated with the lower strata of society and those who are not very well educated and, in some cases, not educated at all.

This association demonstrates a negative attitude towards the non-standard language, Creole (be it English, French or Spanish), which may be illustrated by the marginalisation and unfair treatment of people who are predominantly speakers of Creole.

Also, because many people think that English Creole is bad English, it is not widely appreciated in society even though it is the vernacular. It is considered acceptable in informal situations but not seen as good enough for formal occasions. This negative attitude is demonstrated when Creole speakers try to 'pretty-up' their speech when speaking with people they perceive as affluent or educated or both.

- **Political**

Because of society's negative perceptions of creole languages, many people do not support the standardisation of English Creole and criticise or even condemn bilingual education using English Creole and Caribbean Standard English.

However, politics is one of the main engines for the maintenance of minority languages and the development of non-standard languages.

Politicians have the power to convene groups of stakeholders to plan language policies and see to their implementation.

Some Caribbean countries have already drafted proposals for language development. So far, only Haiti has made Creole one of its official languages. However, this is an indication of how attitudes are changing.

While some politicians share the sentiments of society that non-standard languages have no place in formal settings, others use Creole during political campaigns and sometimes even while bantering with each other during parliament. This improves the acceptability of the non-standard language and shows that there is a place for it in politics just as there is room for it in education.

The twice former Prime Minister of Jamaica, the Most Honourable Portia Simpson Miller, was elected to the position despite speaking predominantly Creole. Even though many people objected to her use of the language and called for her to make an effort to adjust her language, her selection and terms in office are an indication to the Caribbean that Creole speakers can have the same opportunities as speakers of the standard language.

- **Cultural**

Cultural factors have contributed a great deal to non-standard languages being more acceptable today than they were in the past.

In the Caribbean today social columns and cartoons published in national newspapers use Creole, social commentaries and talk shows on radio are in Creole and there are even instances of the news and weather being read in Creole. These are supporting evidence that non-standard languages are functioning in society outside of just being used for small talk.

The fact that today we see non-standard language being used in published literature (novels, poems, plays) and in music (dancehall, reggae, soca, calypso) is testament to the work of cultural icons such as Louise Bennett-Coverley, Edward Baugh, Samuel Selvon, Kamau Brathwaite, Bob Marley and Machel Montano, to list a few. These individuals, through their writing, have helped to promote the acceptance of English Creole in the Caribbean. Their poetry and plays are studied in schools not just in the Caribbean; their lyrics are sung by people who may not even have any connection to the Caribbean outside of going to a concert or purchasing an album.

Many Caribbean countries have literary festivals that allow for performances not just in Caribbean Standard English but also in English Creole. This shows that the same function served by the standard language can be and is served by the non-standard language.

While English Creole has its origins as an oral language, it is increasingly being seen in written form. When writers (poets, novelists, playwrights, songwriters and journalists, among others) use Creole in their writing they are promoting the acceptability of the language.

How to determine and evaluate attitudes to language

A person's attitude to language is how he/she thinks and feels about his/her own language and the language of others.

There is no set language attitude and people's attitudes to language will vary. Language attitudes are revealed through actual behaviour.

Behaviour that reveals a person's attitude to language

- What he/she says about a language
- What language he/she uses in different contexts and with different people
- How he/she reacts to another individual's use of a language
- How he/she treats speakers of other languages
- Whether he/she desires to learn another language or not
- Whether he/she objects to a language being used in a particular setting
- Whether he/she expresses a preference for one language to be used over another
- Whether he/she engages in convergence (makes his/her language similar to his/her audience) when conversing with other speakers
- Whether he/she engages in divergence (accentuates and emphasises the differences between his/her speech and that of his/her audience) when conversing with other speakers

Some questions that reveals a person's attitude to language

- How do you feel about a particular individual based on his/her use of language?
- What language do you think should be the language of instruction/the media/politics/social gatherings?
- What language do you think is appropriate for use in church/prayer/conversations with God?

Exam Tip

In the exam, you might be asked to determine somebody's attitude to language.

Always provide textual evidence to support any claims you make.

Exam Tip

Communicative behaviour is a term you will learn in Module 3. (See Chapter 4.)

A communicative behaviour is a non-verbal action that communicates meaning.

When assessing attitude to language, you may also want to look at the speaker's paralinguistic choices.

These include tone, pitch and body language.

They can help to communicate a speaker's attitude to language as well as to contribute to the overall understanding of the extract.

They are useful in revealing the emotions and attitudes of the speakers.

Exam Tip

These are just sample questions that can lead you to understanding how speakers feel about a particular language.

When you are given a passage to analyse for attitudes to language you can ask some of these questions of the characters in the piece and search it for the response.

Remember that the attitude is revealed through actual behaviours so you will also be looking at what the characters do.

- Would you change your speech to sound more like somebody else? Why or why not?
- What language variety do you use when speaking to your parents/your teachers/your peers/strangers?
- Would you use your mother tongue in responding to questions at a job interview? Why or why not?

Attitudes to language may be positive or negative. Attitudes can also be neutral.

Some adjectives to describe attitudes to language

Positive attitudes	Negative attitudes
Pride	Shame
Loyalty	Disgust
Acceptance	Scorn

While you may not always be able to use a specific adjective to describe the attitude being displayed, you must say if the attitude is positive or negative (this should not be your default response though). However, saying simply that the attitude is positive or negative, even when also using a more specific adjective to describe it is not enough; you must say what makes it so.

Check Your Knowledge

[Speaker's name] has a positive attitude to the use of English Creole. She feels pride in her mother tongue. She believes that it is an acceptable and competent language that is suitable in any situation. This is revealed when she uses Creole to [student describes situation from the text]. She doesn't see the standard language as being superior, in fact she expresses that the mother tongue should be given equal status when she says '[student quotes the text]'.

[Speaker's name] has a negative attitude to English Creole. He believes it has no business being the language of instruction and that using it in educational institutions will only hold students back in later life. This is demonstrated when he says '[student quotes the text]'.

[Speaker's name] believes that anyone who uses Caribbean Standard English is someone of good taste, decency and high standing. This is shown by [student describes behaviour from the text of the speaker towards a speaker of Caribbean Standard English]. On the other hand he feels a sense of shame with regard to English Creole. He believes anyone who uses English Creole is uneducated and does not know how to behave. This is shown when [Speaker's name] says '[student quotes the text]'. [Speaker's name] has a negative attitude towards English Creole and a positive one towards Caribbean Standard English.

[Speaker's name] jokes and gossips with her friends using English Creole but switches to Caribbean Standard English when speaking to her superior at work. This shows she feels that English Creole is suitable for casual conversations with friends but that Caribbean Standard English is more appropriate for interactions with people in authority.

Use of language

This section will remind you how to assess the use of registers, dialects, ranges of formality and other aspects of language in various types of interactive settings.

In the Caribbean, as elsewhere, the language people use is affected by their education, class and the social norms of their community. People vary their language to suit the situation and audience. The existence of two language varieties allows people in the Caribbean greater flexibility in how they do this.

How people express their thoughts through speech or in writing is often based on the level of formality of the situation and what they want to communicate to the intended audience.

Register

Register is the term used to describe the different levels of formality in language.

The level of formality used is very much dependent on the context within which the communicative event is taking place.

There are two basic registers – formal and informal.

Formal register is reserved for professional settings where there is greater adherence to the rules of grammar. People strive to use more standard language with formal vocabulary.

Informal register is reserved for casual settings where the language is more relaxed and open to non-standard forms of language and less formal vocabulary. In speech particularly, it tends to be characterised by incomplete sentences and contractions.

In language situations where there are different language varieties, the standard form is used in formal registers and more of the non-standard form is used in the informal registers.

Dialectal variation can therefore be used in assessing registers.

Remember, though, that register is more than just language variety – it includes sentence structure, vocabulary, tone and other aspects of language.

Register differs based on two main factors:

- the situational context – where the interaction takes place and what it is about;
- the social context – who is involved in the interaction and their relationship to each other.

Notice that the situational context deals with location – where, and content – what; while the social context deals with the audience and participants – who. The social context looks not only at who they are but also who they are to each other.

Although formal and informal registers are the basic forms, these can be further categorised into five levels, each with specific characteristics.

These are:

- frozen;
- formal;
- consultative;
- casual;
- intimate.

Exam Tip

The Module 2 essay item requires you to review a piece of literature, and, among other things, evaluate the participants' use of language. This means that you are to make judgements (form an idea of and comment on) on the language choices made by these participants – the variety used and why; whether they code switch and, if so, why; how formal or informal the language used is and how you can account for this.

Registers

	Register	Characteristics	Examples
F O R M A L R E G I S T E R	Frozen	Definition: A language style that never (or very rarely) changes. It is frozen in time and content. Word order and sentence structure are both fixed. This language is often learned and repeated by rote. Use: Situations related to the law; ceremonies, for example in church.	• Miranda rights • Wedding vows • The Pledge of Allegiance • The Lord's Prayer
	Formal	Definition: The language style used in formal settings. It is usually impersonal and traditional or official. It uses the standard form of the language with formal grammar and vocabulary, often with standard phrases. Use: Formal settings such as in education, parliament and courts; formal correspondence, government documents, academic papers.	• Sermons • Addresses to the nation • Parliamentary addresses • Bills and laws • School lessons and lectures • Pronouncements made by judges • Formal announcements • Journal publications • Professional correspondence
	Consultative	Definition: The language style used for professional discourse. It includes moderately formal language and is used in the discourse between two individuals sharing the relationship of expert and non-expert. Use: Two-way conversations where there is interaction and responses are expected; for the communication of expert advice.	Communication between • superior and subordinate • doctor and patient • employer and employee • teacher and student • lawyer and client • judge and lawyer • counsellor and client • bank manager and customer Also used in newscasts.
I N F O R M A L R E G I S T E R	Casual	Definition: The language style used for communication between friends and peers. The non-standard form of the language may be used. It includes loose sentence structure and informal vocabulary. Slang, vulgarities and colloquialisms may be used. This is 'group' language. One must be a part of the group to engage in this register. It is conversational in tone. Use: For group interaction between peers; informal correspondence.	Conversations between • classmates • team-mates • colleagues Language of • chats • personal emails • blogs • social media posts • letters to friends • text messages
	Intimate	Definition: The language style used for communication between lovers, close family or close friends. It is private and familiar talk. The non-standard form of the language may be used. It may include pet names and endearments. It is also the language style used for communication with one's self. Use: Intimate and personal settings.	Conversations between • spouses • siblings • parents and children • best friends Also used in journal or diary writing.

Remember

You would not use the same register you use with your peers during lunch as with your classmates and teacher during a class discussion, even if you are talking about the same topic.

Registers and appropriateness

People speak differently in different situations and to different people, and this is governed by social convention.

The appropriate register is determined by the four Ws:
- who – the audience and the relationship between the participants (factors that are important include the ages of the participants and their social status);
- what – the topic;
- why – the purpose;
- where – the location.

Appropriate vs Not appropriate

Appropriate	Not appropriate
Context: Social event, lounge Speaker to very good friend 'Yow dog! Glad yu could a come. Long time!' Speaker to prime minister: 'Good afternoon Mr Prime Minister. We are grateful that you could join us.'	Context: Social event, lounge Speaker to prime minister 'Yow Mr PM nof respect fi pass through, zeen!'

In the first instance the register used is casual. The language style and use of slang indicate that they are familiar with each other and they are greeting each other at a social event which all ties into the appropriateness.

On the other hand, using the casual register with the prime minister is under no circumstances appropriate. The casual register indicates a level of familiarity that ought to be reserved for close friends and family. The formal or even consultative register would be the appropriate choice as seen in the second instance in the Appropriate column.

Appropriate	Not appropriate
	Context: At a bus stop Speaker to passer-by 'Sexy princess, give me a talk no baby love. You lookin real good.'

It is never appropriate for anyone to use terms of endearments or language of a sexual nature with a stranger. These are characteristics of the intimate register and can be seen as sexual harassment when used inappropriately. It communicates that the speaker has only mastered the informal register and is not able to make a distinction between the casual and intimate registers. Such speakers commit serious social blunders and offend others.

Appropriate	Not appropriate
Context: Doctor's office Patient to doctor 'Dr Maddison, how critical is this condition?'	Context: Doctor's office Patient to doctor 'So Doc, real talk, right now. Is a life-and-death thing this?'

In the first instance the formal consultative register is being used. It is appropriate for the context and the doctor–patient relationship as well as the nature of the conversation that seems to be taking place.

In the second instance, the speaker is using informal sentence structure and vocabulary and even the abbreviated form of the title 'Doc'. This speaker's style is more appropriate to a relationship that is more casual and familiar.

Appropriate	Not appropriate
Context: Text Athlete to team-mate 'Dely, mi naa go fwd a training later. Mi a go pan a ends.'	Context: Text Athlete to coach 'Sir, mi naa go fwd a training later. Mi a go pan a ends'.

The casual register is reserved for peers such as friends, team-mates, and family members. It is therefore acceptable for the athlete to send a text message to his/her fellow team-mate using that register but his/her coach is different. Even if the coach and team members share a level of camaraderie there should be a level of respect shown in how team members address him/her. It is not the use of the non-standard dialect that makes the register inappropriate but the use of slang and colloquialisms and the general tone of the message which suggest that the coach and the team member are of the same rank or stature. In addition to that, the subject matter – that of being absent from training – is one that requires more formality, even if the message is being sent via a text, which in itself is inappropriate.

Appropriate	Not appropriate
Context: Club meeting Student to faculty advisor	Context: Club meeting Student to faculty advisor
'Miss, please forgive Janeen's attitude. She was just upset because Michael was talking with Lisa during the meeting.'	'Miss don't mind Janeen, she was just **** and had an RBF all through meeting caz her bf was chattin with the lil *** Lisa.'

Similar to the preceding situations, the nature of the relationship between a teacher and a student is formal and therefore requires the formal register in communication interactions. In the first instance the use of the standard dialect, the vocabulary and the sentence structure indicate the formal register and this is a suitable style to use in a student–teacher dialogue.

In the second instance, the student uses abbreviated terms and informal vocabulary which are characteristics of the casual register that would be more appropriate with friends or other club members. This suggests that he/she has no boundaries where relationships are concerned or that for him/her there is nothing wrong with speaking to an adult in the same way he/she would talk to someone of his/her peer group.

Appropriate	Not appropriate
Context: Job application Applicant to personnel manager (her uncle)	Context: Job application Applicant to personnel manager (her uncle)
'Dear Sir, I wish to submit this application for the advertised post of...'	'Hey Uncle Peter, am applying for the job your company advertise in the paper...'

In the first instance the applicant has used the formal register. This is appropriate because she is writing a professional letter which dictates that the style of that letter should be formal.

In the second instance the applicant has used the casual register. This is inappropriate because, despite the fact that the personnel manager – who is likely to be conducting the interview and hiring process – is the uncle of the applicant, their personal relationship does not alter the fact that applying for a job is a professional endeavour and requires the formality that goes along with professionalism. The letter is not being sent to the recipient in his role as uncle to the applicant, it is being sent to him in his capacity as personnel manager and therefore should have none of the intimate and casual register characteristics that are evident in the second example.

Dialects

In the Caribbean where there are two dialects of a language, there is generally a continuum. Speakers in these language situations will vary their dialect to fall at different points of the continuum.

Use of dialect is connected with register because people may vary their dialect based on the situational and social context of the communicative event.

- Dialects that contain exclusively or almost exclusively the features of the standard form are associated with formal registers.
- Dialects that contain a mixture of features of the standard and non-standard forms are associated with less formal registers.
- Dialects that contain exclusively or almost exclusively the features of the non-standard form are associated with informal registers.

To identify dialectal variation, look for differences in pronunciation, vocabulary and grammar, because different dialects have different characteristics.

If the speaker is code switching (moving between one variety and another in the same utterance or conversation) there is dialectal variation.

If there are two speakers involved in the situation and one is using one language variety and the other is using a second there is dialectal variation.

Most people will vary their dialect at some point – people in different everyday situations; news reporters interviewing eyewitnesses and presenting the news; novelists, playwrights, bloggers and television and radio hosts may all use language on different points of the continuum. They do this in response to the various situations in which they are communicating.

Factors affecting an individual's choice of dialect

You have seen that choice of register and dialect is governed by the situational and social context within which language is used. But what other factors might affect an individual's choice of dialect?

Some people may be strictly speakers of Caribbean Standard English and will rarely use Creole; others may be strictly Creole speakers and will rarely or never use Caribbean Standard English.

These are some possible factors.

- Education – How much education has the speaker received? Does the speaker have the capability to speak Caribbean Standard English?
- Familiarity – How familiar is the speaker with the different forms of the language? Does he/she use Caribbean Standard English in his/her job or does he/she rarely hear or speak it? What forms of the language are used where the speaker lives? (People living in the cities are likely to encounter more of the standard form.) What form of the language is used in the speaker's home?
- Economic – Does the speaker have the means to travel? (If so, they are likely to encounter more of the standard form.)
- Status – How does the speaker see him/herself? How do others see the speaker? How does the speaker want others to see him/her? How old is the speaker? How old is the person he/she is talking to?
- Media – What forms of media does the speaker encounter? What forms of language do they use?
- Attitude – Does the speaker accept the social conventions or rebel against them?

Exam Tip

You need to be able to either identify examples to illustrate dialectal variation or to explain the variation, or both.

To do this you need to be very familiar with the characteristics that distinguish Creole and Caribbean Standard English.

Exam Tip

When you are assessing a speaker's use of language there are a number of things to consider.

Remember that the extract given will provide you with the information you need – the four Ws: who, what, why, where.

Use this information together with what you know about dialectal variation, register and the roles of language to make an assessment of the speaker's use of language.

Exam Tip

In the exam, when you are assessing a character's use of language, you must identify the language variety used – whether it is Creole or Caribbean Standard English and you must talk about any variations in dialect.

You must explain why they use the language forms they do.

Your explanation should include:

- the participants' personal circumstances;
- the situational context;
- the social context.

Factors affecting an author's choice of dialect

In the exam you may be asked about the author's choice of dialect.

This may be influenced by what he/she is writing about but there may also be external factors affecting his/her choice such as who he/she is writing for and what is his/her attitude to language.

- The community in the piece would use both Creole and Caribbean Standard English in real life so the author may use both varieties to accurately represent the situation.
- The author may use some or exclusively Creole to appeal to readers who are more comfortable using Creole than Caribbean Standard English.
- The author may use some Creole to celebrate the use of Creole to a predominantly Caribbean Standard English-speaking readership.
- The author may use Creole to promote it as an acceptable language form and a language in its own right.
- The author may use Creole to exemplify it as a literary tool.
- The author may use a mixture of Creole and Caribbean Standard English in an attempt to eliminate the stereotype that one language is superior to the other and show that both languages can accomplish the purpose of communication.
- The author may sometimes use Creole to create a comedic effect and Caribbean Standard English to create a more sombre effect.
- The author may feel more comfortable using Creole because it is his/her mother tongue.

The role of technology in communication

This section will remind you how to

- identify the technological advances that have impacted on communication;
- examine how communication is affected and effected by the use of technology in different cultural settings and interactive contexts.

Technological advances and communication

Advances in technology have changed the way people communicate, making it quicker and simpler.

Here are just a couple of examples.

- smoke signals → messengers from point A to point B → public pay phones → landline telephones → cell phones (unsmart) → smartphones
- letters → telegrams → fax → email

Developments in communication technology

Print
- Paper
- Printing press
- Newspapers
- Tabloids
- Books

Electronic
- Satellite
- Radio
- Television
- Tele/video conferencing
- Telephone
  - Cell phones
  - Smartphones
  - Messaging/calling apps (WhatsApp, Hangout, Skype, FaceTime, Imo, etc.)
- Internet
  - Email
  - Browsers and search engines
  - Digital social networking tools (YouTube, Twitter, Facebook, Instagram, Snapchat, etc.)
  - E-books

The use of technology in communication

Developments in technology have caused a communication explosion. In general, this has had a positive effect on the lives of people across the region.

Obviously, one of the most significant developments has been the invention of the world wide web. However, the development of smartphones and other mobile devices, such as tablets, has enhanced the impact of the Internet, making it available wherever people are, on a 24/7 basis.

A global village

The Internet generally has made the world into a global village. Communication is quicker and easier than in the past and it doesn't matter where in the world the participants in the communicative event are.
- The Internet and cell phones make keeping in touch with family members and friends easy.
- Similarly, it allows business to be conducted remotely. For example, business meetings can happen via video conferencing, with participants remaining in their own countries and documents can be transferred using file-sharing sites more or less instantly. Among other things, this facilitates international trade and homeworking.
- Depending on the platform used, responses via electronic media can happen and be accessible in real time, almost as immediately as face-to-face conversations.
- Emailing is to the present day what telegrams and letter-writing were to the past. With an email you can send a short message to convey a simple thought or idea, or a lengthy, more complicated one. You can add files, images, videos and web page links to your message if you want, similar to enclosing photocopies, photographs, videos, etc. in a letter but with far greater ease and far less expense. Email can eliminate the need for face-to-face meetings.
- Communication can take place with a multitude of contacts across various platforms and services with far less effort than before.
- Employers have access to the most qualified and experienced people in their industry and the access is not necessarily limited to their local area, country or region.

- Businesses have much easier access to their markets and potentially can access much bigger markets. The Internet has transformed advertising and marketing.
- People have access to a greater range of products and services.
- Chat sites and social media allow for conversations and discussions with people who live outside your country or region. Interaction with other cultures makes people more aware of cultural differences. Awareness of the meanings of different communicative behaviours and understanding of different religious beliefs and cultural practices can make integration easier.

Everyday life is easier

- The Internet and related devices, applications and platforms make it easier to accomplish what we want or need to do in life, whether that is to pay bills, buy things, keep in touch with friends and family, date, pitch ideas, source information or store documents.
- Social networking has altered the way people share ideas. It facilitates sharing of photographs, thoughts and videos. The various social media platforms and apps available today enable communication that is effortless, speedy and more frequent.
- Banks are encouraging clients to set up online bank accounts. Government agencies and commercial operations are establishing an online presence for the payment of bills.
- Schools and other educational institutions are encouraging the use of computers and tablets during class sessions and for communication with teachers and lecturers.
- Pitching ideas at work and/or making presentations at school is greatly enhanced by what technology affords, for example PowerPoint presentations and audiovisual aids.

Information is more accessible

- The Internet makes an enormous amount of information available and much of it can be accessed for free. People can access far more information, far more easily than in the past. The opportunities for learning and knowledge expansion are far greater.
- Research projects no longer require trips to a library to find the necessary information through books and magazines. The world wide web allows more information to be accessed and it can be done from the researcher's own home or workplace.
- There is longevity in information posted to the Internet as nothing ever goes away.
- People are connected to the world 24/7 – information is literally at our fingertips. The news is no longer restricted to being reported via newspapers or on the radio or TV. Newspapers and news channels now also post the news on their websites. This has a huge implication for freedom of information. Whereas governments could seek to control news published in newspapers or on the TV and radio, they cannot control news published on the Internet.
- Regional policies are now accessible online so citizens have greater access to information.
- The Internet has opened up the world to people who may not be in a financial position to travel or attend an educational institution overseas through easy access to education websites, podcasts and specialist sites.

- A wealth of information is available via the web and people can self-diagnose illnesses, learn to fix and do things on their own and get ideas for various aspects of their lives. It gives people a greater autonomy.
- People with disabilities can access information thanks to the development of computer programs that are voice- or thought-activated.
- Reading and writing is more accessible to a wider cross-section of people. In this way, technology promotes literacy.

Anybody can have a voice

- Blog pages, social media sites and online journals allow people to publish stories, thoughts, commentaries, videos, music – in fact, anybody can publish anything on the Internet. This has its downside but it allows the publication of articles, books, films, etc. without the need for backing from the traditional outlets.
- Smartphones can be used to record illicit acts and violent crimes. Publication on the Internet allows a greater dialogue with regard to injustice and wrongdoing.
- New careers have been created with the formation of the Internet and social media platforms – bloggers, vloggers, social media managers, social media consultants, social media advertising executives, etc.

The effect of technology on language

Language is dynamic and it evolves through our interaction with technology – print media, television (films, television shows, sitcoms, talk shows, music videos), the Internet and digital devices.

- Development of new words, e.g. 'Internet', 'app', 'selfie' 'to unfriend', 'to tweet'.
- Altered word classes, e.g. 'friend' is just one example of a noun that is now used as a verb.
- Altered meanings, either by expanding or changing the emphasis of a word or by changing its meaning altogether.

   Examples:

   The word 'status' is now used regularly in reference to a status on a social media platform.

   The word 'troll', once used to refer to an unpleasant mythical creature, has been adopted to refer to someone who posts deliberately provocative or offensive comments online.

   The word 'surf' has been given a completely new meaning – to look through information quickly on the Internet – which has only a tenuous connection with its original meaning of riding on waves standing on a special board.

- A whole range of abbreviations and acronyms have been developed to save the effort of typing and to keep within character counts when using written forms of electronic communication, 'CU L8R' = See you later and 'LOL' = Laugh Out Loud being just two examples.
- Emojis have developed to help better convey emotions when communicating through short written messages.
- Similarly, writing messages in UPPER CASE is now used as a convention to indicate that the author is shouting or angry.
- Today when someone is asked for their contact details these are no longer just their name, address and telephone number. Now, in

addition to or instead of a landline telephone number, people will provide a cell phone number; in addition to or instead of a residential address, people will provide an email address. They may also provide a website address and social media URLs and handles.

- The structure of the letter has altered due to the use of email.
- Text messages are beginning to become more acceptable in more formal situations.
- Greater opportunities for language use – people in general but students in particular get to write and share their thoughts using different technologies. This will provide students with different stylistic models which can help them to improve their use of language.

Module 2 Practice questions for Paper 1

<u>Items 1–4</u>
<u>Instructions</u>: **Read the following poem carefully and then answer items 1–4.**

Massa God a fi mi God, di two a wi have an undastandin
And God see and know I wouldn't disrespect him
But Sista Sharon words hat mi fi true
Is patwa wan mi know so what else must mi do

'You cannot speak to God in that awful tongue Miss Clarice
Have some respect and show decorum at the very least'
Doco-wara mah? Is what kinda French shi talking?
Gwan like shi neva born right ya in Jerusalem pakin

Don't worry youself Miss Clarice you know is so Sharon stay
From shi come back from big farin school she eva a act a way
Patwa no good for her again, it lick out a her mind
You just talk your talk to God, Him undastand an respond all di time.

Extract from Charity Barrett 'Between Me an Mi God'

1. What does Sista Sharon's statement 'You cannot speak to God in that awful tongue Miss Clarice' suggest?

   A. Sista Sharon thinks Miss Clarice is rude and disrespectful.

   B. Sista Sharon is prejudiced against Miss Clarice.

   C. Sista Sharon thinks Creole is inappropriate for talking to God.

   D. Sista Sharon thinks Miss Clarice has an awful tongue.

2. For what purposes does the writer use English Creole?

   I. To appeal to Creole speakers.

   II. To create humour in the situation.

   III. To exclude people who think Creole is unsuitable for use in church.

   A. I and II only

   B. I and III only

   C. II and III only

   D. I, II and III

3. The register of the poem may be described as

   A. intimate.

   B. formal.

   C. consultative.

   D. casual.

4. The statement 'You just talk your talk to God, Him undastand an respond all di time' suggests that the speaker believes the language between God and Miss Clarice

   A. has the same characteristics.

   B. is easy to interpret.

   C. has human characteristics.

   D. is mutually intelligible.

Items 5–8

Instructions: Read the following scenario carefully and then answer items 5–8.

Sam: Jonathan party did sell off you nuh Karlene.

Karlene: So mi hear. Paul say even DJ Bigga Vibes was there. Cho man.

Sam: My girl, Bigga Vibes shot up the place man! A him make the party nice.

Karlene: [*Sighs*] Mi really miss out this time. But you know my modda not sending me to no party on school night.

[*The homeroom teacher enters. The girls and their classmates adjust their seats and stand quickly.*]

Miss Potter: Good morning class.

Class: Good morning Miss Potter

[*Miss Potter marks the register in silence.*]

Sam: [*Whispering to Karlene*] A wonder what shi coming with today. By the way, we get no homework?

Miss Potter: Samantha we will start with you today. Please give your views on Calpurnia's dreams in Act 2 Scene 2. What does it foreshadow?

Sam: Ahmm [*clears throat*] well, I believe that Calpurnia was … ah … in tune with her husband … and ahmm … she was a shadow of …

Miss Potter: That's quite enough Samantha! Karlene, do you care to elucidate on that?

Karlene: [*Under her breath to Sam*] 'Elucidate on that' shi weird eeh.
              [*Aloud*] Ahmm … sure Miss Potter. I believe that what Sam was suggesting is that Calpurnia's love for her husband was so strong that she sensed the evil that was lurking around for him and this was manifested in her dreams. The dreams themselves foreshadowed Caesar's end.

5. What feature of Caribbean English Creole grammar does the expression 'my modda not sending me to no party on school night' exemplify?

    A. Consonant deletion

    B. Double negative

    C. Front-focusing

    D. Segment reduction

6. Which of the following is not a factor that influenced Sam's language choices in the scene?

    A. Context

    B. Audience

    C. Social status

    D. Topic

7. The language between Sam and Karlene is appropriate because

    A. they are at school.

    B. they want to exclude others.

    C. they are discussing a serious matter.

    D. they are close friends.

8. Which of the following technologies would help to highlight the various elements of this scene?

    A. Overhead projector

    B. Microphone

    C. Video recording

    D. Flash photography

Items 9–12

Instructions: Read the following letter carefully and then answer items 9–12.

Dear Mista Edita,

I am writing this letter from the bottom of my heart to tell you how proud I am of you and the things you talk about in the paper. I really like how you put a spin on things and help me to understand what and what is taking place in this country. Is about time somebody start write the papers in fi wi language. After all, news a news, the language don't change it. This is a long time coming you know Mista Edita and soon soon the Minister of Education will follow suit and put it in schools. The pickni dem wi learn betta. Anyway, Mista Edita, that is my two cents. It may no worth much but I sell it. Walk good Mista Edita and may good duppy walk with you.

Etc,

Adina Adlam

9. What is Adina's attitude to the use of Caribbean English Creole?

    A. Appreciation

    B. Pride

    C. Indifference

    D. Shame

10. What feature of Caribbean English Creole is exemplified in the expression 'soon soon'?

    A. Metathesis

    B. Reduplication

    C. Compounding

    D. Subject–verb word order

11. The expression 'fi wi language' in 'Is about time somebody start write the papers in fi wi language' is used in this case to

    A. alienate other speakers.

    B. mark a social bias.

    C. mark solidarity.

    D. promote the Creole.

12. Which of the following is NOT a context within which Caribbean English Creole is used?

    A. Between friends

    B. In a political campaign

    C. In education

    D. At a club social (fête)

<u>Items 13–15</u>

<u>Instructions</u>: **Read the following scenario carefully and then answer items 13–15.**

[*Pansy reads the litany of signs in the lobby as she waits to be called for an interview.*]

NO SMOKING IN THE LOBBY.
AN OFFICE LOBBY = A SILENT ZONE.
NO SLEEVELESS, BACKLESS OR STRAPLESS TOPS FOR LADIES.
NO BOTTOM-REVEALING PANTS FOR MEN.

Receptionist: Mrs Raymond, Miss Boyd will see you now.

[*Pansy walks through the open door. She stops. She recognises the person behind the desk.*]

Pansy:	[*To herself*] No Pauline daughter that. [*Smiling brightly, she walks towards the desk.*] Keisha? Is you fi true. My gosh what a way you grow nice. Big office an desk and all these lovely tings.
Ms Boyd:	[*Coldly*] Madam, please, sit. You are here for a job interview are you not?
Pansy:	[*She sits, still smiling.*] Yes Miss Keisha, mam. I feel so proud to see you. Lawd geez. I going to have to tell you modda.
Ms Boyd:	Listen Miz … [*glances down at her clipboard*] Raymond, this is an interview, not a social tête-à-tête.

[*Pansy's eyes pop open. She sits up in the chair, crosses her ankles and puts her shoulders back.*]

Pansy:	Mi apologies Miss Keisha.
Miss Boyd:	Miss Boyd! The name is Miss Boyd. Not Miss Keisha Miz Raymond.
Pansy:	The name is Pansy. *Mrs* Pansy Raymond, *Miz* Boyd.
Miss Boyd:	Listen, Mrs Raymond. I do not know why you believe that we are at all familiar but if you are to work in this establishment, under my employ, you will understand the hierarchical structure of our interaction. Now, may I have the copies of all your credentials and the two letters of reference you were asked to submit.
Pansy:	[*In her head*] But look ya no Jesus. Look pan dis pikni what mi help her mumma raise. Change her nappy and all these tings. Teach her fi walk an use Chimmy.
Miss Boyd:	[*Glaring*] Well?
Pansy:	You know *Miz* Boyd. I doan think this job going to work for me. Yu likle bit too posh an high class fi my taste an I don't want rude to yu. I respect yuh modda too much. So I will keep my credentials and mi reference dem. You can keep you speaky spoky an yu office. Behavin like you don't know me. I know you. You a Pauline daughter from down a Seaside. You forget where you come from but don't forget this – the higher monkey climb the more him expose.

[*Pansy walks out of the office with her head held high and closes the door softly.*]

13. Which of the following are reasons Miss Boyd may insist on using Caribbean Standard English?

   I.   She wants to distance herself from Pansy.

   II. She wants to establish her authority.

   III. She wants to maintain the formality of the context.

   A. I and II only

   B. I and III only

   C. II and III only

   D. I, II and III

14. How does Pansy view Miss Boyd's use of language?

   A. As impressive.

   B. As insulting.

   C. As showing off.

   D. As weird.

15. The phrase 'is you fi true' is an example of

   A. front-focusing.

   B. broken English.

   C. subject–verb agreement.

   D. the phonology of Caribbean English Creole.

Chapter 4

Introduction

Module 3 deals with speaking and writing. As the culminating module, it requires you to incorporate all that you learnt in the two previous modules along with the Module 3 content and apply your cumulative knowledge in responding to the Module 3 questions. There is a lot of content for Module 3 and you are expected to be very familiar with it. In addition to that, you will need to apply your critical thinking skills in using the content to respond to the questions.

For the Module 3 essay, you will be given a stimulus and are expected to produce a response to it. You may be asked to write a speech, an essay, a proposal or even a letter. It is very important that you pay attention to the stimulus as well as what is required of you in the different parts of the question.

The communication process

> This section will remind you how to describe the communication process.

Communication is a process. In order for it to happen, there is a procedure that needs to be followed. To describe the process you need to always remember the elements involved in the process and the role that each plays.

Elements in the communication process

- Sender or encoder
- Message
- Medium or channel
- Receiver or audience
- Feedback
- Context

Describing the process

- **Conceptualisation**
  Communication begins with someone – the sender – thinking about what to include in the message.

- **Encoding and transmission**
  The message is then put in a particular form (written or oral) and transmitted to the receiver through a particular medium or channel.

- **Reception and decoding**
  The audience receives the message and decodes (interprets) it.

- **Feedback**
  The receiver responds to the sender of the message by sending feedback.
  This feedback serves as evidence that the message was communicated, be it effectively or ineffectively.
  Once the original sender receives the feedback, the process can be considered complete.

Objectives

This chapter will help you revise these objectives:

- describe the process of communication;
- apply specific communication concepts to different situations;
- identify the specific features of verbal and non-verbal communication and appropriate contexts of use;
- describe the mental and social processes involved in speaking and writing;
- manipulate non-verbal elements and modes of speech and writing, appropriate to specific purposes and audiences;
- employ appropriate channels (mediums) for specific oral and written presentations;
- use appropriate organising and formatting strategies in producing specific types of oral and written communication;
- describe the uses to which information communication technologies can be put in the learning process.

Note

No feedback is still feedback.

If the sender does not get a direct response from the receiver, it tells him/her that the message was not received or not understood or that some barrier might have affected the process.

The sender can then follow up his/her original message and keep the communication going until the process is complete.

- **Encoding**
  Putting the message into language form – verbal or non-verbal.

- **Medium or channel**
  These two words mean much the same thing.

  The medium or channel is the way in which the message is sent to the receiver.

  It may be by electronic means, printed media, face-to-face communication, etc.

  Examples: newspapers, television, billboards, the Internet (email, social media pages, YouTube, etc.), radio, etc.

- **Context**
  This is two-fold.

  It is situational – where the interaction takes place and what it is about.

  It is also social – who is involved in the interaction and their relationship to each other. Are they friends or strangers? Do they belong to the same language community? Are they from the same cultural background?

Facilitators of the communication process

A facilitator of the communication process is anything that helps the communication process. The aim of communication is for the message to be received and understood.

When talking about how facilitators contribute to effective communication, you need to identify the facilitator and explain how it helps in the process.

Facilitators include:

- **Appropriate message format**
  The format of the message will aid the communication process if it is suitable for the message and the audience.

  Example: if the prime minister of a country wants to address the nation on a current state of emergency, a suitable format would be a speech.

- **Appropriate language**
  The language of the message must be one that is known to the audience.

  The sender must consider the audience's knowledge and ability to decode the text of the message and this should influence his/her choice of words, etc.

  In the Caribbean, the situation is complicated by the existence of a continuum between Creole and Caribbean Standard English.

  The sender must ensure that the language he/she uses is appropriate to the context of the situation in which he/she is communication.

- **Accessible channel**
  For communication to be effective, reaching the target audience is key.

  When choosing a channel, the sender must ensure that the channel is available to the audience and that a message sent by that channel will reach all of the target audience.

  Example: consider again the prime minister addressing the nation. A suitable channel might be television, as this would reach the majority of the nation at the same time. However, if the majority of the population is without access to television or electricity or any of the other elements that enable the reception of television programmes, then this is not going to be a suitable channel and alternative channels need to be considered.

- **Aids that enhance the encoding of the message**
  Audio, visual and audiovisual aids may help to make the message more audience-friendly and easier to understand.
  Examples: microphones, projectors, ICT.

Barriers to the communication process

A barrier to communication is anything that interferes with or hinders the communication process.

Anything that causes understanding of the message to be negatively affected is considered a barrier.

Barriers to communication are often context-specific. Some of the common ones are explained below, but when identifying barriers you will need to look at the communicative context and identify things that may adversely affect communication.

- **Ambiguous message**
  Ambiguity comes in when the message is unclear or if there is more than one possible interpretation of the message.
  It can cause confusion and may result in the message being misunderstood.

- **Inappropriate message format**
  If the message format selected is not suitable for the audience, this will affect how well the message is interpreted.
  Example: if the audience is a group of people who were not exposed to education and who therefore have a reading level below that of a third grader, an inappropriate format would be a letter or any other form of written communication that uses a lot of words since they would not be able to read it because of their level of literacy. A message communicated in this way would be highly ineffective.

- **Inaccessible channel**
  As explained under the facilitators section above, a channel needs to be available and reachable in order for communication to be effective.
  Example: if postal mail is being used as the channel to send a message and there is no postal service where the receiver is or he/she has to commute several miles in order to receive mail, this is likely to adversely affect the communication process.

- **Language barrier**
  If the sender and the receiver are from different language communities, the language chosen for communication needs to be one that is known to both.
  If this is not the mother tongue of either or both the sender and the receiver, this is going to adversely affect communication by affecting the encoding and/or the interpreting of the message.

- **The use of jargon**
  This can be seen as similar to a language barrier. In fact the use of any words not familiar to the receiver will make the message less easy for him/her to understand.

- **Cultural differences**

  If the sender and the receiver are from different cultural backgrounds, in addition to the likely existence of a language barrier there may be additional factors adversely affecting communication.

  Examples: different cultures use body language differently. Additionally, the sender needs to be mindful that some words may have different connotations in different cultures and this may affect how the receiver interprets the message when he/she decodes it.

- **Expectations and prejudices**

  These can affect both the encoding and the decoding of the message, with the result that the message is not received as it was intended.

- **Internal barriers**

  Internal barriers are those conditions peculiar to the receiver that may affect his/her ability to focus on and/or interpret the message accurately or even at all.

  Examples: fatigue, hunger, stress, headache or other kind of pain, hearing impediment.

- **External barriers**

  These are conditions outside the receiver's control that may have a negative impact on his/her ability to interpret the message accurately.

  Examples: actual noise or other distractions in the environment, the speaker having a speech impediment.

Verbal and non-verbal communication

This section will remind you how to

- apply specific communication concepts to different situations;
- identify the specific features of verbal and non-verbal communication and appropriate contexts of use.

Understanding verbal communication

Verbal communication is any form of communication that includes the use of **oral** (spoken) or **written** language.

The message is communicated to the receiver using words.

So we use speech and writing to communicate verbally.

There are four skills associated with verbal communication:

- reading;
- writing;
- speaking;
- listening.

Communication is a step-by-step process that works like a loop.

For written communication to be effective the skills of both writing and reading need to be employed – the sender must write the message and the receiver must read it before communication can be said to have taken place.

Similarly, for spoken communication both speaking and listening skills are required – the sender must deliver the message through speech and the receiver must listen to it in order for communication to take place.

Always remember that context plays a large role in the communication process and as such verbal communication can be either formal or informal, depending on the context.
It tends to be formal:
- when occurring between strangers;
- in business contexts such as meetings, conferences and business negotiations;
- in legal contexts such as court proceedings and parliamentary debates.

It tends to be informal:
- when occurring between family members, friends or co-workers;
- when the subject matter is inconsequential, such as small talk, which can occur even between strangers;
- when there is no structure, no time limit or no topic guidelines to the communication.

Oral communication

On a day-to-day basis we communicate a lot of information orally.

Oral communication consists of all spoken exchanges.

It can occur in a face-to-face meeting of two people or in a manager's presentation to a large audience; you communicate orally with your peers, family and teachers every day.

Oral communication can be formal or informal and it can be planned or accidental.

It takes place just about everywhere.

Examples include interviews, counselling or helping colleagues, meetings, conferences.

Types of oral communication

- **Dialogue**

  Conversations between two or more people.

  They can be either casual or formal.

- **Debate**

  Generally a formal discussion or argument, although there can also be informal debates.

  Generally in politics, educational settings or business meetings in which colleagues may disagree on a point of view or decision.

  The argument tends to be structured – each side is given the opportunity to present a position on the issue.

- **Discussion**

  The process of talking about something in order to arrive at a decision.

  Discussions happen in various settings, for example school, home, the workplace, in the street.

  They can be either formal or informal.

- **Speeches**

  Differs from the other categories by being almost or completely one-sided.

  The sender broadcasts his/her message but may not receive feedback from the audience.

  Speeches can be either formal or informal.

Advantages of oral communication

- Can enable speedy exchange.
- Immediate feedback is possible.
- People can ask questions and clarify points.
- In a face-to-face interaction, the effect of the message on the audience can be noted.
- The sender is able to check whether the message is clear or has created confusion.
- Spoken instructions are flexible and easily adaptable to many diverse situations.

Disadvantages of oral communication

- Depending on the context, it can be time-consuming
- Can be difficult to meet the objective of the communication.
- Poor presentation of the message can result in misunderstanding and undesired responses.
- Spoken communication is influenced by non-verbal communicative behaviour, such as tone and body language, which may affect the meaning of the message in the mind of the receiver.
- Usually there is no record of the communication.

Written communication

Types of written communication

- Books
- Letters
- Emails
- Texts
- Memos
- Notices
- Magazines
- Newspapers
- Personal journals
- Notes

Advantages of written communication

- Written communication is good for complicated and/or vital instructions. They can be given in a precise and uniform manner and they can be referred back to.
- There is less chance of the message being misunderstood.
- Written communication provides a record of the communication.
- Authority is transmitted more effectively with a written order than with an oral one.
- The message can be carefully prepared and then directed to a large audience through mass mailings.
- Written communication can also promote uniformity in policy and procedure and can reduce costs in some cases.

Disadvantages of written communication

- It is impersonal.
- People may not always read written communications.
- There is no immediate feedback.
- It is not possible for the receiver to obtain immediate clarification if they do not fully understand the message.
- It may create mountains of paper work.
- It can be poorly expressed by ineffective writers.

Understanding non-verbal communication

Non-verbal communication is communication that does not involve the use of speech or writing.

It is those wordless cues, which include facial expressions, body language, tone of voice, distance, artefacts, etc., that communicate messages.

Although non-verbal communication can and does work by itself, it is also used in conjunction with verbal communication and can either complement or contradict the message.

You will often find that the terms 'non-verbal communication' and 'communicative behaviours' are used interchangeably. The reason is that non-verbal communication is the use of physical actions and manipulations to convey meaning and so it is considered to be communicative behaviour – behaviour that communicates meaning.

Types of communicative behaviour

Body language

- This is the use of the body (postures and movements), be it conscious or unconscious, to convey attitudes and feelings.
- It includes posture (e.g. slumping at your desk), gestures (e.g. waving), facial expressions (e.g. smiling), eye contact (gazing at someone) and other actions (e.g. yawning).
- The same aspect of body language can communicate different messages. For example, yawning may communicate that the individual is bored or tired; failure to make eye contact may be a sign of shyness, embarrassment, lying or nervousness; making eye contact may communicate brazenness, defiance, an invitation or a challenge.
- Because body language can be interpreted in different ways, it is easy for it to be misconstrued.

Proxemics

- This is the use of space and how it communicates different impressions and meanings.
- Example: a person is sitting on a public bus which is almost empty and the next person who gets on the bus sits right next to him/her. If the first person immediately gets up and moves away, it communicates that he/she is not happy about the other person's behaviour. The other person's choice to sit next to him/her also communicates a lot about how he/she relates to others, his/her interests and his/her type of personality.

Chronemics

- This relates to the use of time – being early or late, keeping people waiting or the use of pauses when speaking.
- Chronemics can communicate a particular attitude or status.
- Examples: if a person turns up early for a job interview this may communicate respect; it may also communicate that he/she is genuinely interested in the job or that he/she really needs the job that is at stake.

    If a young person constantly gets home after his/her curfew this may communicate a lack of respect for the rules set by his/her parent(s).

If a more senior person keeps someone who has made an appointment to see him/her waiting, it could be seen as demonstrating his/her authority.

When politicians are speaking, timing is used throughout the speech to create various effects. For example, they may pause, in order to grab and maintain the audience's attention.

Comedians also use timing a lot as this is important in delivering punchlines that work.

Artefacts

- Any object – a piece of jewellery or clothing or a vehicle – may be used to communicate something about the type of person you are, or that you belong to a particular group.
- As the saying goes, first impressions last. How are these first impressions created? They are created because when you meet someone, you look at him/her and, among other things, you notice the various artefacts associated with him/her. You use what you see to form an opinion about the type of person he/she is. This is, of course, why it is important to dress smartly for a job interview.
- Communicative behaviours, especially artefacts, tend to perpetuate stereotypes. What this means is that we expect a certain type of person to dress in a certain way or to possess or use certain objects.

Paralanguage (vocalics)

- Paralanguage adds dimension and meaning to words.
- Paralanguage is one way in which people reveal emotions and attitudes. It can be conscious or unconscious.
- Paralanguage or vocalics (it is called vocalics because the voice 'surrounds' the words) can be divided into three categories: how people speak, human sounds and interjections.
- People can change, consciously or unconsciously, the volume, tone and pitch of their voices and the speed at which they speak.
- For example, people often raise their voices and shout when they are angry.
- How words are spoken can also be used to clarify meaning. Remember that sentences can be ambiguous, especially because in regular everyday conversation people tend to speak mostly in phrases instead of complete sentences.

    For example, the expression 'Put the bag there' could be a command or a question. The receiver can tell by how the expression is uttered and where the speaker places the stress. If the stress is on 'put' as in '**Put** the bag there!' then it is a command. If the stress is on 'there', as in, 'Put the bag **there**?' and it is spoken with rising intonation, it is a question.
- People can vary the speed at which they speak and this can be used to create an effect. For example, politicians may speak very slowly and deliberately to suggest that what they are saying is of great importance.
- In this highly technological era, paralanguage is also evident in written communication, mostly informal communication via electronic media. By convention, writing in capital letters and/or an increased font size is taken to mean the writer is shouting. Even in the past there was the exclamation mark to indicate emotion such as anger, surprise or forcefulness. In recent times, multiple exclamation marks are used

in informal communications. There are also now emoticons, to aid the expression of attitudes and emotions. All of these things fall under the category of paralanguage.
- Paralanguage also encompasses the sounds people can make. These include laughs, cries and moans. The different sounds have different meanings and communicate different feelings and emotions which people recognise.
- The third category of paralanguage is interjections. These are expressions such as 'oh', 'eh', 'ugh' and 'hmm'. Although they may seem incomprehensible, each has some special meaning whether it is acceptance, agreement, uncertainty, disgust or displeasure.

The five senses
- The five senses (sight, hearing, touch, taste and smell) are used in non-verbal communication.
- Examples: a bad odour on a person may communicate that he/she does not practise proper hygiene, or it could suggest that the person is unwell.
    A particular engine sound in the driveway may communicate the arrival of a family member.
    The sound of a siren in the distance may communicate that there is an emergency somewhere.
    Overly salty, peppered or burnt food by a generally excellent cook may communicate to the recipient the cook's displeasure.

Graphics and symbols
- These are used in different areas to communicate different things.
- Examples: information is often presented graphically to aid in the communication of ideas.
    The periodic table is used in chemistry to symbolically represent the various elements.
    Braille uses patterns of raised dots to represent letters, numbers and words that a visually impaired person can recognise.
    Sign language involves the manipulation of the hands and fingers to communicate with the hearing-impaired.
    Semaphore is a system of communication using two flags held in different positions to represent letters of the alphabet.
    Hand signals, sometimes enhanced with flags, batons, paddles or gloves, are used for directing traffic.

Functions of non-verbal communication
There are six basic functions.
- **Substituting**
Non-verbal communication may be used to replace verbal communication.
    Examples: using head motions to point out someone without saying anything.
    Beckoning for someone to come to you without calling out to them.
    Waving goodbye instead of saying it out loud.

- **Reinforcing**
Non-verbal communication may be used to reinforce or complement verbal communication.
    Example: pounding your hand on a table when arguing to reinforce the point being made.

- **Regulating**

  The regulating function of non-verbal communication is used mostly in conversation to control the flow of messages.

  Example: raising your hand and waiting your turn to answer or ask a question in class.

- **Contradicting**

  Sometimes non-verbal communication is used to contradict the meaning of the verbal communication it accompanies.

  The most common example of this is using vocalic sarcasm – when a person says one thing but the tone of his/her voice tells the listener that he/she means the opposite.

  An example of when the non-verbal communication may unconsciously contradict the verbal communication is when someone states that he/she is attentive to someone while at the same time he/she is looking around or even yawning.

- **Managing impressions**

  Non-verbal communication is often used to manage impressions.

  The most common example of this is the way people dress. A person will often choose to dress in a way which coincides with the impression he/she want others to have of him/her. Dressing smartly for a job interview was mentioned above.

- **Establishing relationships**

  Non-verbal communication may be used to show the sender's relationship with another person or that he/she belongs to a particular group.

  Example: the wearing of a wedding band is a non-verbal indication that the person is married.

Contexts of communication

The context of a communicative event includes what the communicative event is about, why it occurs and where it takes place and the relationships and roles of the people involved.

Communicative events occur on a spectrum from formal to informal.

A formal situation is one where behaviour is dictated by social norms and patterns.

An informal situation is one where there are no constraints on behaviour and communication.

The relationship between speakers influences the context. An employer and an employee discussing a sports report is in a different context from two friends who are discussing the same sports report.

Remember that there are two aspects to context: situation and social.

Situational

- Where the event is taking place, for example at the office, at a bar or in court.
- Why the event is taking place, for example at a party, at a funeral or at a political rally.
- What the event is about, for example, someone's health or the latest sports results.

Exam Tip

Remember you learnt about contexts of communication in Module 2 in relation to registers.

Think about the four Ws: who, what, why, where.

Social

- Who is participating in the event.
- In Module 2 you learnt how people's relationships and their status affects communication.
- The culture to which the participants belong also plays a part in communication. People's cultural backgrounds introduce a broader set of circumstances and beliefs that influence how conversation happens. What happens at a funeral, for instance, differs according to cultural beliefs and practices. In some cultures men and women may not have open dialogue while in others it is acceptable.
- The media influences the cultural context within which people operate as it introduces other cultures into daily life through news, music, films and television programmes, for example. These can impact on how people speak and what they speak about.

Types of communication

- **Intrapersonal communication**

  This is communicating within yourself.

  Examples: thinking, daydreaming, solving problems.

  Hunger, pain and pleasure are messages sent by parts of the body to the brain.

- **Interpersonal communication**

  This is any communication that happens between two or more people.

  Examples of interpersonal communication between just two people include interviews, conversations and intimate communication, but all of the following types of communication are interpersonal communication.

- **Small group communication**

  This is communication that takes place within groups of approximately 3–20 individuals.

  It tends to involve some sort of leadership and is characterised by shared beliefs and norms. Ideas are generally being exchanged among members.

  The small group is one of the most important communication settings.

  Examples of small groups include the family, interview teams, work groups, legislative subcommittees and military and business groups.

- **Organisational communication**

  This is communication that occurs in a business, government or educational context.

  It relates to messages travelling up, down and around a large collection of individuals.

  It may involve any of the other types of interpersonal communication, such as small group, public or mass communication.

- **Intercultural communication**

  This may also be referred to as cross-cultural communication and happens when information is shared between members of different cultures or social groups.

  It is found in any type of interpersonal communication in which an individual communicates with another individual from a different culture.

  It is important to take into consideration the differences between the cultures in order to ensure successful intercultural communication.

- **Public and academic communication**

  This occurs when one person (or more, depending on the occasion) communicates with an audience in either a public or an academic setting in order to deliver a message to that audience.

  Often, the communication is one-way, with one person sending a message and the audience receiving the message, although debates are an exception to this.

  The size of the audience can vary but is generally a large number.

  Examples of public communication include speeches, debates and communication via a town crier.

  Examples of academic communication include essays, research papers and seminars.

- **Mass communication**

  This occurs when information is disseminated on a large scale to a large number of people.

  It is almost exclusively one-way.

  It involves the use of the mass media to transmit information. This includes print (newspapers, magazines and billboards), electrical (radio, television and video) and electronic (computers and phones).

The mental and social processes of communication

> This section will remind you about the mental and social processes involved in speaking and writing.

Communication is a process and it starts with conceptualisation.

This is related to the mental processes of speaking and writing.

First you must think of the ideas you wish to convey, allow your thoughts to formulate and then you articulate them, either in speaking or writing.

The social processes of speaking and writing allow various forms of social interaction between individuals and between smaller and larger groups.

As you have seen, people adapt their communication to suit the context they are communicating in, and this is a social process.

Exam Tip

An integral part of the syllabus is how and why the various aspects of communication are used.

When you are reviewing non-verbal communication and modes of speech and writing, think about their purpose and their suitability for different audiences.

For your portfolio, know how you will tailor these according to the purpose of your presentation as well as the audience to whom you are presenting. Be able to rationalise your choices.

Communicating appropriately

> This section will remind you about manipulating non-verbal elements and modes of speech and writing, appropriate to specific purposes and audiences.

You are expected to not only be aware of the different non-verbal means of communication and modes of speech and writing but also how and when to use them.

When you learnt about these different aspects of communication, you learnt about their purpose and the contexts in which it is appropriate to use them.

Here are just a few examples to remind you what you have learnt.

For instance, if you were asked to deliver the eulogy at a funeral and a candidate's address during a 'student leaders' campaign', you would dress differently for each occasion and your tone of delivery as well as your body language during the delivery of each would be different.

As another example, if you were addressing a group of room attendants in the hotel industry in a rural part of the country, you would not use language that would alienate or offend your audience nor would you use irrelevant technical terms that would interfere with effective communication.

A final example would be if you were applying for a job. You would not do this by writing a text. In your letter of application you would use formal language and much of the standard wording associated with such letters.

Channels of communication

This section will remind you about appropriate channels (mediums) for specific oral and written presentations.

A channel of communication refers to how the sender gets his/her message to the audience he/she wants to communicate with.

Many channels can be used for a number of purposes. It depends on how they are used and the information that is included on them. Some channels are more likely to reach particular audiences.

Exam Tip

The Module 3 question on Paper 2 might ask you about the media/channels you would use to reach a particular audience. Often this is related to advertising.

Oral presentations that have featured on Paper 2 include campaigns, presentations, speeches and addresses. Written presentations include proposals.

Some channels of communication and what they are used to advertise

Medium/channel	Campaigns	Seminars	Presentations	Speeches/ addresses	Proposals
Posters	*	*			
Banners	*	*	*	*	
Billboards	*				
Flyers and brochures	*	*	*	*	
Town crier	*	*			
Interviews on radio or television or in newspapers	*	*			
Announcements on radio or television or in newspapers or as pop-ups on social media sites	*	*			
The Internet (social media, websites and emails)	*	*		*	
Articles in newspapers (national, school); newsletters (community, clubs)	*	*			
Celebrity endorsement	*	*			
Debates and discussion					*
Lectures		*	*		

Medium/channel	Campaigns	Seminars	Presentations	Speeches/ addresses	Proposals
Workshops	*	*			
Dramatic presentations			*	*	
Concerts	*				
Jingles	*	*			
T-shirts and other promotional items	*	*		*	
Slides	*	*	*	*	*
Film and documentaries		*	*	*	
Face-to-face interaction	*	*			

Note

It is possible to combine different channels with the various media. For instance, you can post flyers on social media sites or have local celebrities talk about your event on radio or television.

Using channels of communication

Posters, banners and billboards
- Once strategically placed, posters, banners and billboards can reach a large audience.
- They need to be placed in high-traffic areas which are frequented by the audience you want to attract.
- They are good for reaching students as you can place them in the school or college they attend.
- They can be used to disseminate information or to lure people to a function or event.
- Posters, banners and billboards can stick in the minds of viewers and so the purpose needs to be considered carefully when they are being designed.
- They can be relatively cost-effective.
- Another good point is that you can have several of them in one area or in close proximity, which will increase visibility.
- If you want viewers to take some action, for example, attend an event, volunteer their services, make a donation, don't forget to include that on the poster.
- If you're promoting to teenagers or young people, the posters and banners need to be bold, colourful and catchy. More graphics (cartoons, emoticons, etc.) and pictures may be used. For an adult audience, you still want attractive posters because the idea is to grab attention, but you may want fewer emoticons and pictures.

Flyers and brochures
- Flyers and brochures are also very easy to prepare and can be produced in large numbers.
- Whilst brochures are mainly used for passing on information, flyers are multifunctional and may be used both to pass on information and to promote events.
- Flyers and brochures should be easy to read and attractively designed so that they will grab the audience's attention.
- Flyers and brochures allow you to give more in-depth information than is possible with posters, banners and billboards.
- They may enable you to get feedback that can further help your purpose.
- Brochures given at an event have the benefit of recapping information given at the event and can also provide additional information that may not have been covered.

Town crier

- A town crier has the ability to jolt listeners because announcements are loud and persistent. The town crier forces the target audience to pause what they are doing and take notice, so they are likely to hear the information being conveyed to them.
- The town crier uses repetition and may visit one area several times. This constant replay helps to make the information stick with the audience, so much so that after a few trips the hearers are able to follow the announcement and even repeat it along with the town crier.
- The town crier is an effective way to reach a large number of people from a particular locality.
- It is one of the few ways of reaching audiences that lack access to mass media or who are unable to read.

Mass media

- Mass media includes newspapers, TV, radio and the Internet. They have the potential to reach a large number of people.
- Using mass media really helps to get your information out to your audience and can be used whether your aim is to inform, encourage or promote.
- A downside can be cost. To actually place an advert may be expensive but there are ways to get a message on mass media without placing an advert. For example, you could get an article about a campaign in a newspaper or give an interview about an event on the radio. Information can be disseminated via social media free of charge if you have the ability to reach your audience in this way.
- Most people access at least some of these different kinds of medium, often several times every day. It is important to consider which are most accessed by your target audience and when they are accessed.
- When it comes to using television as a means of communication the aim is to push your content during the timeframe that you know your target audience is likely to be watching. That way you can capture and engage their attention.
- People listen to the radio in their cars, on buses or in taxi cabs on their way to and from work, school or other places, and so communication via this medium is also very effective.
- The Internet allows for communication to take place at just about any time and any place. Through smartphones, tablets and laptops on the go or via a computer, audiences can access information at any time. You can provide up-to-date information to your audiences, which helps to keep your content current and relevant.
- Using social media is a particularly effective way of reaching teenagers and young adults as this group are particularly heavy users of this channel.
- Effective use of mass media relies on you knowing the habits of your target audience.

Celebrity endorsement

- Local celebrities are useful as a medium of communication at seminars and campaigns. They might be musicians, artists, actors, sports men and women or TV personalities.
- They are very effective in promotions. People are drawn to celebrities whom they admire and may want to emulate, and they are therefore more likely to listen to what they have to say.

- For example, if you are having a seminar about healthy lifestyles or organising a campaign to promote them, having a sports star speak on the topic will get your audience to pay attention and listen.
- The presence of celebrities may also be used simply to encourage your target audience to attend your event.

Debates, discussions, lectures, workshops, dramatic presentations and concerts

- These are all channels that can be used in different kinds of presentations as well as for different target audiences.
- Debates and discussions allow you to pass on information to the audience as well as engage them in an active forum where they can share their ideas, ask questions and give feedback. They really facilitate interaction, which enables you to determine whether your purpose is being achieved and allows you to modify your message accordingly if necessary.
- Lectures are better for more mature audiences and are suitable only for particular topics – largely academic ones.
- During seminars and even campaigns you can use workshops as a means of communication. They have the benefit of having your audience directly involved in what is taking place and this can help to keep your audience engaged and interested. Being directly involved in a particular process will also enhance memory so your audience is likely to leave your seminar with the information you wanted them to have. Also when people are directly involved in something they are more likely to feel they have a vested interest in it and so if your aim was to get their involvement in a cause then a workshop can help to pull them in.
- Dramatic presentations are fun and entertaining and can be used to capture the attention of a diverse audience. They can be used for education as well as promotion and because they utilise so many non-verbal means of communication along with the verbal, the messages being conveyed are enhanced. The nature of dramatic presentations captures and maintains the attention of the audience, which makes them very effective as a means of communication.
- A concert can be used as a channel for communicating information. During a campaign, for instance, you may have a concert during which you may have performances of songs, poems, stories and dramatisations which pass on information to your audience. This might be new information or reiterate information already presented. Local celebrities can be incorporated here as they can be involved in giving performances.

Jingles

- Jingles are catchy and easy to remember. Once your audience hears a jingle a few times, the information sticks in their consciousness.
- Jingles are generally used for promotion and are shared via the Internet, radio or television. They are especially effective when they are performed by celebrities. This way the target audience is more likely to pay attention to the information being shared through the jingle.

T-shirts and other promotional items

- Although T-shirts and other promotional items are not conventional mediums of communication they can be very useful.

- You can put information on T-shirts, cups, pens, notepads or other tokens that you can give to audience members as memorabilia for them to take away from your seminars, campaigns or speeches. You can also wear the T-shirts during your presentation so that the audience has a visual image of your theme or slogan, whichever you choose to put on the shirt.
- These tokens are keepsakes and so, unlike a flyer for instance, which may be read (or not) and then immediately discarded, people are more likely to hang on to them, which means your message stays with them.

Slides, films and documentaries
- Slides, films and documentaries as mediums of communication are helpful as they provide visual or audiovisual aids which can help to retain audience attention.
- During an oral presentation incorporating slides, films or documentaries may help to re-energise the audience.
- They can also be used to provide additional information or clarification for the audience.

Face-to-face interaction
- With face-to-face interaction there is a direct line of communication between yourself and the target audience.
- Each party gets to exchange information – you not only get to share information with your target audience but the audience is able to make queries and you are able to provide explanations that can clear up any misunderstandings.
- It provides immediate feedback and this immediacy creates the opportunity for improvement. For example, you can focus on members of the audience who do not appear interested, to try to convince them of the merits of your promotion.
- You are better able to build rapport and, out of that, develop relationships with your target audience and ultimately trust. This will result in a greater level of cooperation and support.

Organising and formatting strategies for oral and written communication

This section will remind you how to use appropriate organising and formatting strategies in producing specific types of oral and written communication.

Organisation and formatting is the structural framework of your speech or writing. It is all about how you put your information together to ensure that your presentation – be it oral or written – is coherent, easy to follow and captivating.

Some types of written communication that may be required of you:
- letter
- memo
- proposal

- bulletin
- advertisement
- brochure
- poster
- report
- essay (academic, college admission, personal statement)

Some types of oral communication that may be required of you:
- speech
- presentation
- lecture
- interview
- video conference
- podcast
- VoIP (Voice over Internet Protocol, e.g. Skype, FaceTime, etc.)

For both oral and written communication, the introduction (how you begin) and the conclusion (how you end) are important.

Review these two elements of organisation in Chapter 5.

Also remember that in the introduction you want to capture and captivate your audience and in the conclusion you want to leave them on a high and remembering the essence of your information.

The writing process

In order to properly prepare for written and oral communication, remember to engage in the writing process. Through the process you will make choices on how best to organise and format your information.

Steps in the process

Prewriting
- Brainstorm – think of and jot down all your ideas on a topic.
- Create a visual picture of your ideas where you group all related ideas together – you could use clustering or semantic mapping.
- Create an outline.

Drafting
- Put your ideas into sentences and paragraphs.
- Expand and explain your ideas.

Revising
- Review your original and subsequent drafts – focus on audience and purpose and make amendments as necessary.
- Consider these questions:
  - Does it come across as if you are speaking directly to the audience?
  - Is the information clear and concise?
  - Do you have enough evidence to support what you say?
  - Have you defined all relevant terms and given all necessary information for ideas to be understood?
  - Do your ideas flow as a cohesive unit?

Exam Tip

Chapter 5 gives you advice about how to write the answers to the items in Paper 2.

You will find more detail about the writing process there.

Editing and proofreading

- Check your work and make corrections where necessary.
- You are checking for:
  - grammar and mechanics;
  - spelling – you can and should use the computer to check your spelling but be aware that it doesn't tell you if you have used the wrong word.

General organisation skills

- Begin with a hook.
- Develop the middle using appropriate organisational strategies.
- End with a bang.
- Connect ideas (sentences and paragraphs) using relevant and logical linkages.
- Create focus and emphasis:
  - Define the scope – outline the objectives and what needs to be done in order to achieve these objectives.
  - Streamline:
    - Prepare opening lines.
    - Offer positive reinforcement.
    - Use appropriate vocabulary.
    In written communication:
    - List any personal details of the addressee that you will use in the communication.
    - Write as if you are talking to the reader.
    - Stick to one main topic – stop when you are finished.
  - Emphasise your central ideas using literary devices – you want to ensure that the devices you use draw attention to the idea you want at the centre.
  - Highlight important information so it stands out:
    - Consider using bold, italics, underlining.
    - Present figures using charts and graphs.
    - Consider using different font styles and/or sizes, particularly for headings.
  - Think formatting:
    - Use a succinct title and subheadings.
    - Consider incorporating bulleted points.
    - Use short sentences to give details about data.
    - Use extra space between paragraphs and bulleted points.
    - Consider breaking the page into columns.

Don't forget that different types of communication will have different organising and formatting styles; some have traditional styles that you must adhere to, like a letter, a report or a memo. Refresh your memory by reviewing these styles.

Information communication technologies and the learning process

This section will remind you about the uses to which information communication technologies can be put in the learning process.

Information Communication Technology (ICT) is a broad area and involves using computers, television, radio, telephones and the Internet. The various information communication technologies can be further categorised accordingly:

Input
• Computers and laptops
• Tablets and iPads
• Document readers
• Application software
• Word processors
• Web browsers
• Spreadsheets
• Database programs

Output
• Projectors
• Interactive whiteboards
• Television

Other
• Digital cameras
• Digital recorders
• Smartphones
• Digital books
• Films and videos
• Audio clips

Uses of ICT

ICT is very useful in the learning process. It can be used in developing writing, thinking and speaking and presentation skills. Each ICT device has its own use, which determines its contribution to the learning process.

With the aid of ICT it is easier to conduct research, analyse findings and produce documents.

ICT and writing skills
• Write posts for blogs, status updates for social networks, posting and responding to tweets, commenting on articles and news items on the Internet.
• Create a web page for a particular content area and have written interaction between classmates and teachers – students can give feedback and post comments.
• Create an online journal.
• Design and create different products.
• Make notes when conducting research, and summarise findings.
• Access different kinds of writing styles.

ICT and speaking and presentation skills
- Help with explaining concepts.
- Enhance retention of ideas.
- Make presentations interactive.
- Make it easier for participants to follow a presentation.
- Create visual aids to emphasise a point or add detail.
- Help to generate ideas.
- Show slides and transparencies.
- Create podcasts with classroom news.
- Record students' work.
- Allow for webinars.
- Have videoconferences or teleconferences with experts sharing views.

Other uses of ICT in the learning process
- Multimedia and storytelling
- Simulation exercises
- E-books
- Assessment
- Publishing work
- Virtual activities
- Global learning environment
- Animation, simulations and models
- Web research
- Demonstration

Module 3 Practice questions for Paper 1

<u>Items 1–3</u>

<u>Instructions</u>: Read the following scenario carefully and then answer items 1–3.

Tanisha is always nervous in front of strangers. There is a group of US exchange students sitting in her Communications Studies class for observation and this has affected Tanisha, who needs to do her mock expository speech.

1. Which of the following communicative behaviours would suggest that Tanisha is indeed nervous?

   I.   Fidgeting

   II. Lack of eye contact

   III. Profuse sweating

   A. I and II only

   B. I and III only

   C. II and III only

   D. I, II and III

2. What non-verbal cues can her classmates use to help her to relax?

   A. Whispering and giggling

   B. Thumbs up and giggling

   C. Silent staring

   D. Smiling and nodding

3. Which of the following elements in her speech would contradict her nervousness?

   A. Voice trembling

   B. Hasty speech

   C. Voice strong and firm

   D. Breathlessness in delivery

<u>Items 4–6</u>
<u>Instructions</u>: **Read the following scenario carefully and then answer items 4–6.**
You are the president of the environmental club at your school and you are asked by the principal to run a recycling campaign called 'Reviving Plastic'. Your job is to make the school populace aware of how they can help in this venture.

4. Which of the following are appropriate means of encouraging students to take part in the recycling campaign?

    I.   A skit in devotion

    II. A devotion sermon on cleanliness

    III. Posters

    A. I and II only

    B. I and III only

    C. II and III only

    D. I, II and III

5. Which strategies could be used on the school's website to spread awareness?

    I.   Use of a catchy tune

    II. A voice-over on recycling done by a local celebrity

    III. 'Did you know' cartoon pop-ups on the homework and general info portal

    A. I and II only

    B. I and III only

    C. II and III only

    D. I, II and III

6. What register would be most appropriate for the messages sent out to the student populace?

    A. Intimate

    B. Casual

    C. Formal

    D. Frozen

Items 7–10

Instructions: Select the most appropriate answer for items 7–10.

7. Which of the following is not a function of non-verbal communication?

   A. Substituting

   B. Reinforcing

   C. Explaining

   D. Managing impressions

8. How can 😠, 😀 and the use of 'lol' rather than 'LOL' be classified?

   A. As vocal fillers

   B. As artefacts

   C. As injections

   D. As paralanguage

9. Which of the following are elements of the communication process?

   I. Encoding

   II. Interference

   III. Feedback

   A. I and II only

   B. I and III only

   C. II and III only

   D. I, II and III

10. Which of the following would NOT be a barrier to communication?

   A. An accessible channel

   B. An unfamiliar language

   C. An inappropriate medium

   D. An ambiguous message

Items 11–12

Instructions: Read the following scenario carefully and then answer items 11–12.

Oraine is suffering from the flu and cannot go to school. His mother writes a letter to the principal and sends it in the mail. The letter did not get to the principal until after Oraine had returned to school a week later.

11. Which of these methods would it also have been appropriate for Oraine's mother to use to communicate with the principal in this case?

   I.   Email
   II. Text message
   III. Phone call

   A. I only
   B. II only
   C. I and II only
   D. I and III only

12. Which of the following BEST explains why Oraine's mother sent a letter?

   A. She doesn't know how to send an email.
   B. She is old-fashioned and prefers writing letters.
   C. She wanted a record on Oraine's file.
   D. She felt the principal would understand a letter better.

Items 13–15

Instructions: Read the following scenario carefully and then answer items 13–15.

A Communication Studies teacher is very upset with her class. The speeches they delivered during the mock presentation the week before were poor. She tells the class that the speeches were disjointed, lacked structure and contained inappropriate grammar. She places students into groups of three to review each other's written speeches and give feedback on how to improve them.

13. What part of the process should students be working on in their groups?

   A. Introductions and conclusions

   B. Revising and editing

   C. Brainstorming

   D. Formatting and linking ideas

14. Which kinds of communication context are evident in the scenario?

   I. Intrapersonal

   II. Interpersonal

   III. Small group

   A. I and II only

   B. I and III only

   C. II and III only

   D. I, II and III

15. What communication technologies can be utilised during the presentations to make their speeches better?

   A. Projected slides and video clips

   B. An iPad with the written speech

   C. A television

   D. A microphone to aid projection

Chapter 5

Techniques for Paper 2

Objectives

By the end of this chapter you should be able to do these things:

- write with effective control of grammar, vocabulary, mechanics and conventions of writing in the use of Caribbean Standard English;
- evaluate examples of written and spoken communication, taking into consideration the form and content of the communication and the context in which it is presented or constructed;
- apply comprehension skills of analysis and critical evaluation to a wide range of oral and written material;
- present information in speech and writing with precision, accuracy, clarity and fluency;
- demonstrate competence in organising written communication;
- write well-structured content for each item on Paper 2.

Note

These are the marks and timings that have been used in relation to this course but always double check with your teacher and/or the syllabus in case they change.

Introduction

This chapter focuses on various techniques that you can use when preparing for your exam, as well as when responding to the three Paper 2 items.

In order for you to optimise your marks in each section, you must present a balanced script – balanced in terms of content as well as how you present that content.

This chapter is a 'how to' chapter that will help you to strike the right balance when writing your responses.

You will be given guidelines on how to plan and structure your essays as well as various checklists – for language, content and organisational structure for instance. While going through this chapter you should be able to apply the content that you have reviewed in the previous chapters in drafting a coherent, well-organised and error-free response to any exam question asked.

Your overall aim is to produce answers that are precise, accurate, clear and fluent. To this end, there is an exam-style question with a sample answer for each module and, at the end of the chapter, a practice question for each module.

General pointers

- Content and use of language complement each other.
- If your content is comprehensive but your organisation and expression are weak, your marks will be affected.
- Similarly, if your organisation and expression are excellent but you are lacking in content, you will not be able to maximise your marks.
- Each essay is worth 25 marks.
  Marks for the Paper 2 essays are allocated as follows:
  - Content: 10 marks
  - Organisation: 7 marks
  - Expression: 8 marks
- You have 2 hours and 30 minutes to write the three essays – that is 50 minutes on each one.
- Practise answering exam questions or exam-style questions in the time allowed.
  Count how many words you have written and use this to see what 90 words, 350 words and 500 words look like in your handwriting.

Writing the Paper 2 essays

There are three items on Paper 2, one on each of the three modules.

The items on Modules 1 and 2 require you to write an essay.

The item on Module 3 does not always require an essay, so careful review of the item is necessary to determine the required format.

An essay must always have:

- an introduction;
- a body;
- a conclusion.
  Other formats often have this structure too.

Introduction

- This can be as few as three sentences.
- Highlight key elements in the questions posed to you and comment on what you are writing about.
- Present a thesis – make a general statement that captures the various parts of the question to which you are responding.

Body

- Use the sections of the question to organise the body of your essay. If the question has three parts, then the minimum number of body paragraphs you will need is three.
- Think of each body paragraph as a mini-essay.
  - Introductory sentence – write a sentence that reflects the part of the question you are answering.
  - Developmental sentences (body) – in the next couple of sentences, present points with evidence from the extract to support your point. Be sure to explain fully what you are saying.
  - Concluding sentence – write one last sentence that sums up the answer you just gave; alternatively, write a sentence that reinforces your point.

Conclusion

- This too can be as few as three sentences. The idea here is to give a summary of the ideas and points that you have discussed.
- Rephrasing is key. You don't want to be repetitive and just say the same thing in the same words.
- Write a few sentences that reiterate the points you discussed in the body of the essay.
- End by restating the topic and concluding sentences of all your body paragraphs – preferably in one or two sentences.

Planning your essay

- Plan your essay before you start. Remember the drafting stage you did in process writing? Use that skill.
- Create an outline so that you know exactly what you will be putting in each paragraph.
- Your essay should have between five and seven paragraphs – definitely no fewer than five.
- How you organise your essay can make the difference between a good grade and an excellent grade or between a poor grade and a good grade.
- Remember that 7 of the 25 marks are allotted to organisation.
- You should be aiming for
  - an excellent and effective introduction;
  - thematic cohesion;
  - appropriate and logical use of transitional devices;
  - an excellent and effective conclusion.
- To achieve thematic cohesion each paragraph should develop **one** idea. Do not discuss different parts of the question in the same paragraph and do not begin to respond to part of the question in paragraph 2 and then continue the response in paragraph 5, for instance.
- Use your linking words and phrases within the paragraph to connect your ideas as well as to transition from one paragraph to the next.

> **Note**
>
> Present the points in the same order in which you will discuss them in the body of the essay.
>
> Use the sections of the question as a guide.

> **Note**
>
> The aim is to answer a question and to do so effectively.
>
> So, always review both the question and your answer to make sure that you have fully answered the question asked.

Linking structures and transitional devices

- Emphasised in the syllabus is the need for cohesion – internal cohesion and cohesiveness between paragraphs.
- You achieve this by using linking structures and transitional devices. These may be words, phrases or even sentences.
- In this section you are provided with a list of such words and expressions. This list is not exhaustive, so consult with your teacher and utilise any available resources to ensure that you are familiar with a wide variety of choices.

To add or extend an idea

- additionally
- again
- also
- and
- besides
- by the same token
- even more so
- finally
- first/firstly
- further
- furthermore
- in addition
- in the first place
- in the second place
- last/lastly
- moreover
- next
- or/nor
- second/secondly
- too

To show contrast

- a clear difference
- after all
- and yet
- at the same time
- but
- despite
- however
- in another way
- in contrast
- in spite of
- nevertheless
- nonetheless
- notwithstanding
- on the contrary
- on the other hand
- otherwise
- the antithesis of
- though
- yet

To make a comparison

- by the same token
- correspondingly
- coupled with
- in a similar fashion
- in like manner
- in the same manner
- in the same way
- likewise
- similarly

To express a causal relationship

- as
- because (of the fact that)
- being that
- consequently
- due to (the fact that)
- for
- for that reason
- on account of
- since

To show an effect or result

- accordingly
- as a result
- because (of this)
- consequently
- for this reason
- hence
- in consequence
- so much so that
- so that
- therefore
- thus

To clarify
- I mean
- in other words
- that is
- that is to say
- to clarify
- to explain
- to put it another way
- to rephrase it

To emphasise or intensify
- above all
- besides
- by all means
- certainly
- especially
- essentially
- even more so
- more importantly
- of course
- particularly
- surely
- undoubtedly
- without doubt

To show sequence
- afterwards
- at this point
- at this time
- before this
- finally
- first(ly), second(ly), third(ly)
- following this
- hence
- next
- now
- previously
- simultaneously
- subsequently
- then

To summarise or conclude
- all in all
- as a final point
- at last
- finally
- in brief
- in conclusion
- in short
- in sum
- in summary
- in the end
- in the final analysis
- lastly
- to conclude
- to sum up
- to summarise

To illustrate or to give examples
- as an illustration
- for example
- for instance
- for one thing
- such as
- to demonstrate
- to enumerate
- to illustrate

Managing your writing

Once you have written your essay you need to **proofread** it.

Your aim is to produce an error-free script that demonstrates a superior use of language.

Your language should show maturity and an advanced vocabulary.

You can earn up to 8 marks for your expression and use of language.

Checklist: grammar, mechanics, usage and vocabulary

Ensure that your essays have:
- ✓ Correct spelling
- ✓ Subject–verb agreement
- ✓ Consistent use of tense
- ✓ Pronoun antecedent agreement

✓ Varied sentence structure
- A combination of simple and complex sentences.
- Vary the length of your sentences but avoid overly long sentences that obscure clarity.

✓ Appropriate word choice
- Spend time improving your vocabulary so that you will have a wide repertoire of words from which to choose.
- Remember words have denotative and connotative meanings.
- Be conscious of homophonous words and other words that are often confused – when you proofread, check to ensure you have used the correct word.

✓ No sentence fragments or comma splices (run-on sentences)
- Remember that all sentences must express a complete thought.

✓ No wordiness or redundancy

✓ No misused punctuation
- The comma and the semicolon are often misused – review correct usage leading up to the exams.
- Practise using a variety of different types of punctuation.
- Pay attention to apostrophes.
- Avoid contracted forms.

✓ No clichés or colloquialisms

✓ No vague expressions

The Module 1 essay

General format

The Module 1 question generally comes in two, sometimes three, parts.
- Part (a) will ask you to state the writer's main idea or to give a summary of the writer's main idea in a given word limit (usually 30 words but you should check).
- Part (b) will ask you to write an essay in which you identify the writer's purpose and comment on the organisational strategies and language strategies and/or techniques in a given word limit (usually 500 words).
- If there is a part (c), it will require you to evaluate the piece for reliability and/or validity or to comment on the appropriateness of the writer's tone.
- Sometimes the part (c) component is included in part (b). Whether it is separate or included in part (b), if you are asked for this extra information, it must be included in the essay in its own paragraph. The only section that may be isolated from the essay is part (a).

The writer's main idea and purpose

When writing a Module 1 essay, it is critical that you remember what distinguishes the writer's **main point** (or **idea**) and the writer's **purpose**.

The main point is **what** the writer is writing about; the purpose is **why** he/she is writing about that 'what'.

> **Note**
>
> Use the word limits as a guide to how much you need to write.
>
> Thirty words means you are only expected to write a paragraph; 500 words means you need to write an essay.

> **Note**
>
> There is no penalty for including part (a) in the essay.

How do you identify the main idea?

Ask yourself, 'What is this piece about?'.

Your answer to that question should formulate your response to the main idea.

For instance, if you were to tell your classmates the main idea of this chapter, you might say:

> <u>The main idea of this chapter is that</u> there are various techniques which may be applied to writing effective answers for Paper 2.

Pay keen attention to the lead in; that is the section that is underlined. This is of utmost importance as it shows that you know the distinction between the main idea and the purpose.

How do you identify the writer's purpose?

Remember: the **purpose** is the reason or intention or motive.

Ask yourself, 'Why has the writer produced this piece of work?', 'What is his/her motive?', 'What does he/she want to accomplish?', 'What does he/she want to happen subsequent to reading the piece?'.

Your response should lead you to a **verb**.

For instance, once you complete this chapter we want you to apply the techniques learned to write effective essays for Paper 2. Therefore, in explaining the purpose of this chapter to your classmates you might say:

> <u>The purpose of this chapter is to equip</u> students with the relevant techniques needed to write essays of superior quality for Paper 2.

Note the difference in the way in which you express the main point as opposed to the purpose:

The main point/idea **is that**

BUT

The writer's purpose **is to + verb**

Language techniques and organisational strategies

Remember that different discourse types will employ different kinds of language techniques as well as different kinds of organisational strategies.

Never forget that writers use techniques and strategies in order to convey their main point or to achieve their purpose. Therefore in talking about the various techniques and strategies you must show this correlation.

* Before you begin to plan the essay – in fact, before you even read the given passage – read the question carefully, several times if you need to.

  Underline the key aspects and number your tasks.

> (b) Write an essay of 500 words in which you discuss [1]the writer's purpose and comment on his/her use of [2]language techniques and [3]organisational strategies to achieve this purpose.
>
> (c) Comment on the effectiveness of the [4]writer's tone in achieving his purpose.

Note

Language techniques and organisational strategies were reviewed in Chapter 2. See the section on Discourse types, starting on page 17.

- Then you read the passage.
  Be sure to have a pencil in your hand.
    As you read, underline strategies and techniques that jump out at you.
    Write the names of the techniques and strategies in the margins.
    Also as you read, try to determine the discourse type and make a note of that too.
- Read the passage a second time. This time with greater focus in order to gather the information you need for the essay.
    Remember, time management is important and so an integral aspect of doing well is organisation and planning. So, as you read this second time, read with these three questions in mind:
  - What is this piece about?
  - What is the writer's objective?
  - What techniques and strategies has he/she used to achieve this objective?
  As you discover the answers to the questions, make a note of them.
- After you have done that, review your notes and make a short and simple outline of what you will be putting in each paragraph. Then begin to write.
    Remember the essay guidelines given at the start of this chapter.

The N-I-E principle

When you are discussing techniques and/or strategies you must do three things:

1. Name
2. Illustrate
3. Explain

Everything you write about **must** be specific to the extract given on the exam paper.

Name the technique/strategy

Firstly, you must name the technique or strategy used in the extract.

Examples:

One technique employed by the writer is conversational tone.

Tautology was among the strategies used by the writer.

Illustrate the technique/strategy

Once you have identified the technique or strategy, you need to illustrate it.

    Do this by providing an example or two of its use in the extract given. This is where you write it out.

    Do not say 'for example in line 20' and leave it at that.

    You **must** write out the expression, phrase or sentence that exemplifies the technique or strategy you have identified.

Example:

Tautology is seen in the writer's constant repetition of the idea of death. In line 15 he says 'we take our last breath and we die'; then in lines 21 to 23 he mentions death twice, claiming that 'when death comes for us, we pass away into the other realm' and that 'death is not the enemy of life; life is the foe with which death tangles'.

Explain its use

Then, you explain its use.

This is where you talk about how well the technique or strategy worked in helping the writer to achieve his purpose.

This explanation must refer to effectiveness. In other words, you need to explain the value or helpfulness of the particular technique or strategy you have identified.

Ask yourself, 'How does this device help me to understand the writer's purpose?' or 'How is it helping the writer to put across his/her main point?'.

Example:
The writer uses tautology to emphasise death's constant presence. It draws our attention to the fact that death is an inescapable reality which projects the writer's main idea and helps him in encouraging readers not to fear death as it is an inevitable end.

Another example:
One technique employed by the writer is conversational tone. This is seen in her use of various personal pronouns as well as the anecdotes included in the piece. The former is seen in lines 4 to 6 – 'Have you ever gone to a tourist destination and just felt wowed by everything? Of course you have. Yes you! You have had it. I have had it. We have all, at least once, had that experience. One that left us breathless. You know what I am talking about.' Then the writer follows this with an anecdote about her visit to Antigua, sharing her first vision of the island, the memorable reception she got and how a bell boy tripped over his own leg in an attempt to bring all her bags at once. The writer's conversational tone, found in her use of the personal pronouns, creates a connection between me as a reader and her, the writer. Both the personal pronouns and the anecdotes draw the reader into the piece, causing the readers to feel as though we are directly involved. It makes the piece more relatable and actually makes us as readers want to share in the experience of the visit to Antigua. This is, in fact, the writer's purpose.

The structure of the essay

Introduction

Remember that the aim of an introduction is to acquaint your audience with the topic of your discourse – what you will be talking about.

Go back to the question and formulate a general statement that captures what the extract is about and what the question requires of you.

- discuss [1]the writer's purpose
- comment on [2]language techniques
- [3]organisational strategies to achieve this purpose.
- Comment on the effectiveness of the [4]writer's tone in achieving his purpose.

Example:
In the extract, 'The Signs Tell More Than They Say', the writer focuses on the various hidden messages in things that happen around us and the importance of being able to recognise the messages. His purpose is to evangelise the people and get them to accept that there are alternative beliefs that, if accepted, can save humanity. To achieve this purpose he uses a number of language techniques together with various organisational strategies as seen throughout the piece. His rather sardonic and yet empathetic tone also helps to facilitate his purpose.

Formulate a thesis statement – this does not need to be complex.

It can be as simple as:

This essay seeks to discuss anecdotes, contrast and repetition as language techniques and listing a series of events, cause and effect and a continual forecast as organisational strategies as well as the writer's tone in relation to how these contribute to the writer's purpose.

Another example:

Language techniques such as anecdotes, contrast and repetition, used in conjunction with carefully thought-out organisational strategies, such as listing a series of events, cause and effect and a continual forecast, together with the writer's tone, as evidenced in this extract, help to ensure that the audience understands the purpose, follows the line of argument and will ultimately concede to the writer's desires.

Remember

Use the N-I-E principle.
Name
Illustrate
Explain

Body

This is where you expand on the ideas in your thesis statement.

You will need to explain how the language techniques, organisational strategies and tone that you have identified helps the audience to understand, follow and accept the writer's purpose.

Remember what was stated earlier – you must name, illustrate and explain.

You will already have named the techniques and strategies and identified the tone in your thesis or general introductory statement but you will need to name each in turn as you discuss it.

Example:

The writer's use of anecdotes was useful in helping the reader not only to understand how meanings can be obscured through daily happenings but also how these meanings may be deciphered.

Go on to illustrate and explain the use of the technique or strategy as described on page 116.

Do this for each one.

Remember to discuss each technique or strategy separately.

You may choose to discuss the language techniques together in one paragraph.

If you do this, it must still be properly organised.

This means you discuss one technique before moving on to the next and you use transitional devices appropriately.

Do **not** discuss techniques and strategies in the same paragraph.

Bear in mind your purpose for this essay – to show how the writer uses the three elements – language techniques, organisational strategies and tone, in this instance – to achieve his purpose – in this case, evangelising his audience.

Conclusion

You are now at the end of your essay. You have said all you need to say and now you must sum up the essence of what you said.

One way to conclude:

- Restate the main idea of your essay or thesis statement – that language techniques, organisational strategies and tone are all essential elements in the writer's quest to achieve a particular purpose.
- Summarise the sub-points – that he used a number of techniques and strategies, including … which helped to …
- Make a statement to indicate whether the writer's purpose was achieved. Link this to everything you discussed.

An alternative way to conclude:
- Make a general statement about how the writer's use of language techniques, organisational strategies and tone works.
- Indicate whether the writer's use of the various strategies, techniques and tone were effective.

General pointers

- Do **not** organise your essay based on the paragraphs of the piece. In other words, do not discuss all the techniques and strategies that the writer uses in the first paragraph of the extract and then all the techniques and strategies that the writer uses in the second paragraph, etc.
- **Do** discuss how one technique or strategy is used throughout the extract in each of your body paragraphs.
- If you are not told how many techniques/strategies to discuss, aim to discuss about three.
- State what you are going to discuss in the introduction.
  For example, 'Three language techniques used in the extract are rhetorical questions, historical data and reference to authority.'
      Then, in the body of your essay, discuss each of these in relation to how and why the writer uses them.
- Do **not** define the techniques or strategies.
  For example, you are **not** required to say what tautology is; you **do** need to provide examples and an explanation of its use.
- Remember you have a word limit. Ensure you answer what is required by the question and keep within the word limit. You may not be penalised for a going a little over the word limit, but if you exceed the word limit by more than 5–10% you may lose some of the marks allocated to organisation.
- Bear in mind that you are writing an essay. Do **not** use headings, letters, numbers or bullets to section your response.
- Remember to use transitional devices.

Worked examples

Read the extract below carefully then answer the question that follows.

Dr Watson, I Presume?

Everyone has heard of the famous Doctor Watson of Sherlock Holmes fame, but what about Watson, the world's greatest artificial intelligence (AI) doctor? Created by computing giant IBM, an AI system called Watson recently saved a Japanese woman's life. Her doctors were stumped by her form of cancer. She wasn't recovering quickly enough from their treatment, so they decided to enlist Watson in their fight to save their patient. According to *The Japan Times*, Watson took just ten minutes to find a different treatment plan for the woman that would have taken the doctors two weeks to complete. With cancer, fast treatment is vital. With such amazing results, will Watson take over from human doctors soon?

Watson thinks faster than any human doctor. Doctors rely on years of training and their own impressive, but limited, memory capacity. If like the Japanese cancer patient, you have a rare form of cancer, the doctor may spend lots of time researching and refreshing their memory on your unusual condition. Watson, however, can immediately access tens of thousands of studies, as well as medical records from hospitals all over the world. It can also pinpoint things related to a patient's specific biology. For example, if a person has genetic mutations, or changes, that affect their health, Watson can quickly compare the world's existing knowledge against that patient's needs. It is an incredibly specific tool, tailoring its diagnosis much more efficiently than any doctor.

Most experts say that, although Watson is very impressive, they believe that the flesh and blood doctor shouldn't worry just yet. Patients like the human contact of another human being. Watson cannot, for instance, do a physical examination. As artificial intelligence, Watson cannot express empathy or understand the behavioural cues of patients. Artificial intelligence systems like Watson are very good at mathematical equations and mining data. Unfortunately, they have a harder time clueing into the intentions of the patient, determining whether or not a patient is lying and anticipating how a patient will react to bad news. Imagine Watson trying to console a patient who's just been told they have a terminal, or life-ending, disease? Most experts agree that for these reasons, doctors are not being sidelined any time soon.

Those medical professionals who are already using Watson say it provides the perfect marriage between man and machine. Doctors who use Watson believe that it is a wonderful tool to help them become more efficient in their jobs, and it reduces the cost of healthcare in the process. *Fortune* magazine spoke recently to doctors using Watson for oncology, or cancer, care at some of the world's leading hospitals, such as Mayo Clinic in Minnesota, USA, and Memorial Sloan Kettering Cancer Center (MSK) in New York City. In these hospitals, doctors work with Watson, feeding it all the information they know about a patient. Watson then lists all the potential treatments for that patient. At the end of the process, the doctor makes the final decision on what treatment path to take, in consultation with the patient.

With so much potential to save lives, Watson is an exciting development in the world of medical technology. Though it is early days, Watson has already been improving lives not just in the world's major cities, but also in poor, rural areas where it can be difficult to get high-quality healthcare. Whether doctors like it or not, technology like Watson looks set to stay. Most doctors, like the rest of us, are trying to figure out and take advantage of a new relationship with computer systems that can enhance our jobs, and our lives.

a. In about 30 words, outline the main idea of the article.

b. Write an ESSAY of not more than 500 words in which you make reference to

   (i) the writer's purpose

   (ii) the strategies and language techniques used

   (iii) the effectiveness of the strategies and language techniques identified in (ii) above in achieving the writer's purpose.

Total 25 marks

Main essay

a.   The main idea is that Watson, an AI system, is a remarkable development in the world of medical science, and is already proving to be beneficial to the profession, saving precious lives.

b.   The extract, 'Dr Watson, I Presume?' brings an interesting tool, the Watson AI, to our attention. The AI introduces a more dynamic approach to the medical profession and as the writer states, adds efficiency and improves lives. The writer skilfully utilises various strategies and language techniques throughout the extract in order to achieve his purpose.

The writer's purpose is to inform the reader of this latest development in medical technology, the Watson AI, and show its benefit to modern medicine and encourage its acceptance in medical practice.

In order to properly achieve this purpose, the writer skilfully employs the use of certain organisational strategies. One such is the use of evidence/reference when the writer mentions the woman with a rare case of cancer and then states that 'According to The Japan Times, Watson took just ten minutes … that would have taken the doctors two weeks …'. This reference grabs the attention of the reader as we are already told of the amazing results that Watson is capable of producing and helps us to right away form a positive impression of this artificial doctor. In addition to that, the reference to The Japan Times makes the writer's information all the more credible. The writer also employs the use of examples. By giving us several examples of what Watson is capable of performing in paragraph 2, the writer further emphasises his point that Dr Watson is very beneficial to the medical profession thus effectively contributing to the purpose.

In addition to these strategies, the writer also used certain language techniques. One such technique is juxtaposition. The writer very skilfully places 'Watson' and ordinary human doctors alongside each other in order to show Watson's superiority. The writer shows how quickly and efficiently Watson performs as opposed to a human doctor who is limited by his human capacity. Through the use of juxtaposition here we are able to get a full sense of Watson's capabilities and make a value judgment on just how essential Watson is in this field, thus contributing to the writer's purpose. In addition, there is the use of rhetorical questions in the extract as exemplified by, 'With such amazing results, will Watson take over from human doctors soon?' This forces the reader into deep thought, essentially drawing their attention. Even the title of the piece is stated in a rhetorical question – 'Dr Watson, I presume?' This question is posed to suggest that Watson's capacity and capabilities are so valuable that one day soon he will be very commonplace and one

Left margin annotations

This is the student's response to part (a). Note the lead-in. Remember that this is how you introduce the main idea. It helps to show that you are able to distinguish the main idea from the purpose.

As for indicating the main idea, there is standard wording for stating the writer's purpose: 'the writer's purpose is to + verb'. Note that the student again used the standard wording, further demonstrating his ability to distinguish main idea and purpose.

Remember to use transitional words and phrases to ensure that you create a cohesive unit.

With this transition, the student creates a link between the preceding paragraph and this one and also points out that the information outlined in this paragraph relates to the writer's purpose.

This is the topic sentence. Remember to always write one. It introduces what the paragraph is about.

Think of the paragraph as a mini essay and organise it accordingly.

You need to apply the same principle (N-I-E) for all strategies.

Here the student mentions that the writer provides examples (name) then points to paragraph 2. This is suggesting that the examiner should go to the extract to see the example. This is a NO–NO. As the student, you need to take relevant examples from the extract and include them in your essay.

Transition.

This paragraph illustrates the N-I-E principle throughout.

Right margin annotations

This introduction is brief and effective. It tells us just enough about the passage and then indicates what will be discussed in the essay.

Always aim to have your introduction give a synopsis of the extract then a general statement that captures the requirement of the question – this may serve as your thesis statement if you do not write one separately.

Here the student has outlined the writer's purpose. Although it is clearly outlined, it is presented by itself – as a paragraph. This may well cost him a mark in organisation because at this level it is expected that a paragraph will be well developed and consist of more than one sentence.

To avoid this you can combine the purpose with another aspect of the question.

Note that the question says to write an essay in which you make reference to – therefore you do not necessarily need to separate the different parts. Your response to each can be interwoven but in a clearly organised pattern that is easy to follow.

N-I-E – Name, Illustrate, Explain. This is what the student has done here. He has stated what the strategy is (name), then provided an example from the extract (illustrate) and then explained how the strategy worked in relation to writer's purpose (explain).

Topic sentence.

Here the student did not present a quote as his illustration from the extract, instead he paraphrased based on what is in the passage, which is quite acceptable.

Transitional phrase.

This tells the reader that you are at the end of your discussion and this is the culminating paragraph.

can expect to be seen by him when one goes for a regular doctor's visit.

In the final analysis, in a world where high-quality healthcare is essential in order to save lives, Watson's contribution or rather, potential to save lives cannot be emphasised enough. It is an excellent tool, displaying the highest level of efficiency. In the extract, the writer fulfils his purpose of educating the public about the abilities of the AI machine. This was possible due to his effective use of a combination of organisational strategies and language techniques to bring out his point.

This is the student's concluding paragraph. No new ideas were introduced. The student made a statement relating to the main idea of the extract then indicated that the purpose was achieved and how.

Note, there is no set way to write your conclusion. You just need to ensure that you summarise your points and thesis without being repetitive.

Contributed by: Shamar Wedderburn, Kingston College

The Module 2 essay

Exam Tip

Always read the question first.

It gives you a sense of what to look out for as you read the extract.

The Module 2 essay seeks not only to test your knowledge of the module but how well you are able to apply the knowledge.

For this module the exam question is based on an extract from a narrative passage, a play or a poem.

The pieces selected generally use a mixture of Caribbean Creole and Caribbean Standard English. You are expected to read the piece and respond to the question given.

General format

- The Module 2 question generally comes in two or three parts, but sometimes it may have four parts.
- You are to respond to all the parts in a single essay of no more than 500 words.
- The question focuses largely on the use of language and language varieties (Caribbean Creole and Caribbean Standard English).
- The other requirement of the question is generally one that relates to the use of technology.

Use of language and language varieties

Note

This should be very familiar to you as you would have had practice completing similar tasks for your IA.

To respond to this question you need to be able to comment on any or a combination of the following:
- Attitudes to language.
  - How language use/choice reveals attitudes.
  - How reaction to language use/choice reveals attitudes.
- Ways in which language is used.
- Social factors which influence language choice (e.g. location, occupation, education, status).
- Use of language in relation to social status.
- Motivation for choosing a particular language variety.
- Motivation for wanting to attain a particular variety.
- How choice of a language variety creates tension or conflict.
- Differences in language varieties used (phonology, syntax, vocabulary, etc.).
- Relationship between use of language and the context within which it is used.
  - How context influences language choice.
  - What is the relationship between the people involved?
  - What was their motivation for their language choice?

- What language varieties used reveals about characters.
- Relationship between verbal and non-verbal communication.
- Appropriateness of language variety used.
- Features of the language that would make it difficult to understand for a non-Creole speaker.
- Reasons for the writer's language choice.
- What the writer achieves by using a particular language variety – Creole in particular – and how such a use assists with the advancement of Creole.

You may also be asked to discuss any or all of the following:
- communicative behaviours (e.g. body language);
- use of registers (formal, casual, consultative, etc.);
- dialectal variation (Caribbean Creole and Caribbean Standard English).

Use of technology

The question may require you to discuss:
- how a video recording or televised reading may enhance the piece or any (named) aspect of the piece, such as:
  - communication (verbal and non-verbal)
  - tension
  - conflict
  - discomfort
  - attitudes to language;
- how a televised reading or presentation may enhance meaning;
- how any other (named) technological device may enhance communication, aid meaning, etc.

The structure of the essay

Introduction

- Look at all the parts of the question and ask yourself what you know about what the question requires of you.
- Make jottings.
- Review your jottings and write a few sentences that capture what the question is asking in a general sense.
  That is, write a few sentences that sum up your jottings on what you know about what each part of the question is asking.
- Then write your thesis statement.
  For this, attempt to rephrase what the question is asking into a statement.
    Alternatively, make a general statement about the question.

Body

- Use the sections of the question to structure the body of your essay. Respond to each section in its own paragraph but do **not** label them a, b, c, etc.
- Use transitional phrases or sentences to connect the different paragraphs.
  The beginning and/or end of each paragraph should show how it relates to the one before and/or after it.

Note

Non-verbal communication is covered in detail in Module 3 but you may be required to discuss it in the Module 2 essay. Remember it may also be referred to as 'communicative behaviour'.

Remember

You have to write an essay. It therefore requires three parts: introduction, body and conclusion.

Remember

Your introduction should not be long. It is just a simple road map.

Get to the point in two or three sentences, four at the most.

Remember

There are 7 marks available for the organisation of your essay.

Review the section on linking structures and transitional devices (see page 112) to help you achieve these marks.

- Each body paragraph must begin with a topic sentence that introduces what that paragraph will be discussing.

    Example:

    There have been many technological advancements, all with different advantages to communications; the television for one, if used effectively, can enhance communication in several ways. In this piece for instance, …

- In discussing each section of the question, ensure that there is supporting evidence from the extract to support your claim or perspective.

    Use the I-E-I-A principle (see below).

- Remember that there needs to be cohesion within each paragraph as well as between each paragraph.

- Each body paragraph must end with a concluding sentence that summarises what that paragraph discussed.

    Example:

    Essentially, the television as a technological device would effectively convey the characters' varying attitudes to language as well as the tension involved in the social circumstances of their interaction.

The I-E-I-A principle

In Paper 2 you are expected to demonstrate a high level of analysis.

You can use the I-E-I-A principle to analyse text.

Identify

Explain

Illustrate

Analyse

For example, if the question asks you to comment on attitudes to language:

- First, **identify** the attitude.

    Example:

    Tobie has a rather antagonistic attitude towards the use of Standard English.

- Then **explain** what you mean.

    Example:

    He is very aggressive and hostile to anyone who speaks or attempts to speak Standard English to him and always reacts in a negative manner.

- Then **illustrate** your point by providing evidence from the extract.

    Example:

    One instance of his antagonism is seen in his interaction with his girlfriend Jubie when she came home excited to share her news with Tobie.

    'Darling yu see all dese lovely gifts I does gat at work today. Heverybody were telling me how they like how I make the hoffice wa'm an welco…'

    Tobie slaps the machete on the table. 'Yu hear mi se yu nat to bring yu dam backra talkin into mi house. I not tellin yu again inuh' he warned shaking the machete at her.

- Finally give your **analysis**.

    Example:

    Tobie's attitude suggests that he has no regard for the language that Jubie presents, which he sees as Standard English. His reference to it as 'backra talkin' indicates that he thinks Standard English belongs to the white man's world. He does not feel that this language is a part of his identity and it would possibly make him feel disloyal to his ancestry if he were to tolerate its use. This is why he gets so upset and lashes out when it is used around him.

Conclusion

- This is the grand finale of your essay. You want to recapture the important points you made in the body of your essay.
- Start by making the transition from the last body paragraph. You should signal that this is the conclusion of your essay.
- Rephrase your thesis and main points.
  Select the topic sentences from each of the body paragraphs and rephrase them into one or two sentences that summarise the ideas.
- Do **not** simply repeat the thesis and/or topic sentences.
- Close with a sentence that wraps up everything.

General pointers

- The question in this section is specific to the extract given.
  Do **not** include random discussion to demonstrate general knowledge of the syllabus content.
  You are expected to show how you can apply that knowledge to the questions asked in relation to the extract given.
- Candidates tend to regurgitate definitions of 'mesolect', 'basilect', 'proxemics', etc.
  This is **not** required.

Worked example

Read the extract below carefully then answer the question that follows.

It was 10:30 at night and the big jukebox was at the corner of the street strumming out the cool tones of the Reggae Icon himself. Maas George did love him some Bob Marley. In the yard where the nine-night was actually being held a steel pan band was adding to the rhythm of the night and all the people from the district were milling about the yard engaging in dominoes, card pack and chit chat. Even a cockfight was going on around the corner. In the kitchen a little off to the left of the house, Janet, Babz and Tanya congregated around a humongous wood fire as they chatted up a storm.

'How di mutton comin on, eh gyal?' Fire Stick, the district 'long-belly', shouted to Janet who was stirring the big pot of curry goat with a piece a pimento wood.

'I mighta lick yu in yu ass. You no ear I tell you not to call mi no gyal. Me is big oman fi yu ino. Yu tink me is yu madda? Renk!'

'Aai, no mind Faiya Stick Janet man, cho,' Babz rebuffed, handing Fire Stick a bowl of manish water to soothe Janet's response.

'Good night Mr Fire Stick. I see you are still henkering around our kitchen. Nice bowl.'

That was Josina, Maas George's youngest child.

'Still henkering!' Tanya mimicked as all three women burst into a chorus of belly laughter.

'Come ya Gad,' muttered Janet, still laughing but ignoring the young girl. She never did like Little Miss Hoity-Toity.

'Aunty Babz, could I have just two small cups of the goat soup and is there any of the roasted breadfruit left over from earlier, my fiancé is feeling somewhat famished.'

'But si ya! Manish waata an ruos bre-fruit! Bout yu 'goat soup and roasted breadfruit'. A we yu tink you de pikni?' Yu big farin school?' hissed Janet.

'Janet!' Tanya scolded and pointed to the door with her lips.

Janet looked around to see Stephen, the fiancé in question. She hissed her teeth and went back to stirring her pot.

'Good heeveling, Mr Stephen. I just waamin up the nice goat soup for you with some roasted breadfruit and pickle fish.'

'Pickle fish? Woi, Gad if a laugh in ya tinait I get fat,' chortled Janet. 'Aye Tanya, mine ou you dish out di pikle fish, yu no waan bone juk yu,' she continued as Tanya hurried past Babz to share the food.

'Henjoy di heevling yu hear,' Tanya crooned, handing a small tray to Stephen and a small foil-wrapped package to Josina. 'So you finish the eulogy, Miss Josina?'

'It's Josi now and yes. Well, thank you and we'll see you ladies at the funeral in the marrow' she said as she hooked her free arm through her fiancé's free arm and waltzed off towards the house.

'Den a wa fly up in a your head, Tanya?' Janet could not wait a moment longer to enquire.

'You need fi learn fi behave yuself, Janet man,' Tanya hissed back.

'Mi ma! Den no you did a trouble the child no too long bout "still hankering" an now you see farin people, yu a twang. Yu tink dem beta dan fi hear wi patwa?!'

'I wasn't twangin, mi was a taak prapa. Mi kyaan si nice nice high skin people an chat tu dem boogoyaga like a unu mi a taak to.'

Extract from 'Nine-Night Jamboree' by Charity Barrett

In an ESSAY of not more than 500 words, discuss:

a. the relationship between context and language choice;

b. the attitudes to language of any TWO characters in the extract;

c. how a televised presentation of the piece would capture the atmosphere presented in the extract.

Total 25 marks

This serves as the student's introduction.

Note there is no hard and fast rule as to how the introduction should be written. However, it must satisfy the criteria of pointing out what you will be discussing and in what order.

Remember to be as concise as possible without compromising the requirements.

For this introduction the student:

- states the title of the piece and the name of the author (this helps to create background);
- identifies the language varieties used in the extract as well as the context of the extract;
- says what she will discuss.

This summarises the different parts of the question in one general statement.

One factor that influences language choice is context. In Charity Barrett's 'Nine-Night Jamboree' the language choices are Creole, mostly in the basilect variation, and Standard English, both being used in the context of a wake/nine-night, which is a casual setting. The language used by the characters in this setting reveals various attitudes to language. All of this will be discussed in addition to how a televised presentation of this piece could capture the atmosphere of the extract.

The context or setting plays a vital role when choosing a language. In the extract the context is a nine-night/wake at the home of a deceased friend.

Using a topic sentence clues the examiner in to what you will be discussing in the paragraph.

Everyone's writing style is different so you may not write your topic sentence similarly to another student; just ensure that you have one.

This speaks to organisation.

Here the student outlines the setting – which is necessary.

You cannot merely say the setting was casual or formal. You need to point out the aspects that make it so.

What is outlined here speaks to the relationship between the context and language choice.

What is missing, however, is evidence from the extract to support her claim that the variety used is 'English Creole in the basilect variety for the most part and some mesolectal variation'.

Remember you should always give supporting evidence from the text.

This topic sentence captures what the paragraph will be about. However, it leaves this section of the essay a little disjointed.

Remember that internal cohesion is very important as it speaks to organisation. You therefore need to link each paragraph to the one that went before. This link can be very simple, for example 'Like context, attitudes to language and language choice are related.' Right away you indicate to the examiner the fact that you will be talking on a new point but it's not an entirely new essay.

Like this student, you need to comment on the attitude.

Try to bring a high level of analysis to your response.

This is a good topic sentence. Notice that it provides a link to the preceding paragraphs.

This is good. She has highlighted what the situation is and identified aspects of the atmosphere that will be captured via the presentation, however she has not said what the atmosphere is. This statement 'convey the atmosphere' may beg the question – what is the atmosphere?

Some of the remaining friends are joking and teasing each other. All of this creates a casual setting. Since the context is casual and the characters are familiar and comfortable with each other, the writer uses casual language which is English Creole in the basilect variety for the most part and some mesolectal variation. However, although the setting was casual, one of the characters chose Standard English as her language choice, possibly because of her background and relationship to the others. Additionally, the story itself is narrated mostly in Standard English which may be due to the fact that a story is a formal type of writing and the writer is writing for both a foreign and a Caribbean audience.

Creole is considered to be a backward and broken down form of language which is mainly used for informal settings/situations whereas Standard English is held in high esteem; these views are attitudes to language and speakers of the two varieties identified will have different attitudes. The extract captures the attitudes of both Tanya and Janet towards Standard English and Creole. Janet has an attitude of intolerance towards Standard English whereas Tanya has the opposite attitude. For instance, Janet chastises Josina for speaking Standard English and corrects her in Creole: 'But si ya! Manish waata ... yu tink you de pikni? Yu big farin school?' This suggests that Janet sees Standard English as a put on and that it does not belong in their setting. She doesn't seem to have much regard for speaking Standard English and considers it to be 'twanging'. This is seen when, after Josina leaves she mimics Josina and suggests the she is not better than patwa. On the other hand, Janet's attitude towards Creole is one of pride as she uses it with everyone at all times. In contrast, Tanya's attitudes vary. Her use of language implies that Standard English is the 'proper way' to talk to people of certain class or status while Creole is suitable for friends and company. This is proven in her response to Janet: 'Mi kyaan si nice nice high skin people an chat tu dem boogoyaga like a unu mi a taak to.' These varying attitudes reflect only a few of the attitudes held by people in society.

The various attitudes and the interaction between the characters can be brought to life through a televised presentation, which would capture the atmosphere in this written piece well. The presentation of this can highlight the interactions between the characters as well as the setting they are in, thus enhancing their communicative behaviour. The audience would be able to see the festive scene of the nine-night with all the different activities as well as the camaraderie between the different people. This and the sound effects would help to convey the atmosphere. It would also show the tension between Tanya and Janet while Josina is a part of the scene and bring into focus the facial expression of Janet as she criticises Josina and afterwards pounces on Tanya about her language. The audience would also be able to hear how possibly comical Tanya sounded when she was 'twanging'

Here the student speaks to social context (relationship between participants) to account for language choice.

The student mentions that the language choice for narration is Standard English. This is a good point.

Many students forget that the writer's/narrator's language is a part of the extract and ought to be considered in a question such as the one being answered.

The question asked you to discuss the language attitudes of two characters. Therefore, you must name the characters whose attitudes you will be discussing and it is useful to say to which language(s).

Again you must identify the attitude. You cannot discuss an attitude without saying what the attitude is.

You should aim to explain clearly what the attitude is, as here.

This is an illustration of the attitude. You need this. It is evidence for your claim.

Note the linking structure providing a transition between one point and the next.

Remember to use them within the paragraphs as well as between them.

Here she gives examples from the extract, which are always needed.

She is helping the reader to visualise exactly what will be seen through a televised piece.

This is what needs to be done – you say the audience will hear different tones and you name them.

If you had space, you could give an example of the use of one.

Transition – again, very necessary and appropriate. It signals that this is the final paragraph.

Notice that this paragraph does not introduce any new points. Neither is it merely a regurgitation of what was said previously.

It captures all the student spoke about and how it was done.

– 'Good heeveling'. It would also help the audience to hear the different tones – humour, derision, censure, amusement – that were used in the extract. All in all, a televised presentation would bring the extract to life as the audience can clearly see the setting as well as the characters in real time. To conclude, the languages were chosen for the extract because of the nature of the piece and the audience, as well as the casual setting and relationships of the characters. These language choices further communicated the various attitudes of the characters. Essentially the language used, character interaction and relationships as well as the language attitudes would be highlighted if the piece were to be televised.

Contributed by Sadé Rodney, a graduate of St Andrew Technical High School

Exercise

This essay handles the question really well except for the fact that it exceeds the word limit. (It is about 750 words long.)

The student would score well for content and expression but, although the essay is well organised, she may lose one or more marks for being over the word limit.

Could you write this amount in 50 minutes?

Look back at the student's essay. How could you revise it to make it fit within the word limit?

Exam Tip

Be sure to focus on the requirements of the question.

If the question specifies that your answer should be in essay format, write an essay!

Do **not** write a speech if it is not required.

Do **not** draw a poster if it is not required.

Remember that the techniques for writing a speech differ from those for writing an essay.

Exam Tip

It can't be emphasised enough – be sure to focus on the requirements of the question.

Sometimes the question requires that you create a communication, such as a speech.

At other times, you have to write about the communication process as it applies to the particular context.

There can also be two parts to the question so that you have to do both.

The Module 3 essay

- This section requires that you think and apply your knowledge not only of the Module 3 content but also of the content of the other two modules.
- You may be expected to write a speech or a proposal or some other kind of extended writing for which you will have to create content. Think about the writing process to help you.

General format

- For this module you will be given a scenario.
- In response to this you will often have to write a proposal that relates to the scenario. Other possibilities include a speech or a letter.
- You may be told to discuss specific features of communication.
- Usually the instructions indicate that your response should be given in essay format. Sometimes, a different format is specified.

Exam topics

The context you are given in the exam will, of course, differ each year. However, it is useful to think about what aspects of communication you might have to discuss.

- Strategies used to appeal to different audiences and justification for the strategies.
- Use of language varieties, registers and vocabulary and how you would vary these for different audiences, with justification for the differences.
- Tone to be used with different audiences and justification for this.

- Mediums for presenting and/or promoting campaigns, explaining why these would be appropriate to the target audience(s).
- Channels you would use to reach the audience, explaining why these would be appropriate to the target audience(s).
- Verbal and non-verbal elements that can be used to enhance a presentation.
- Visual aids and ICT to enhance presentations to different audiences.
- Communication challenges that may be faced with a particular group.
- How knowledge of the communication process can help.
- How you would evaluate a campaign.

Writing the answer to the Module 3 question

- Whether the question says 'in an essay' or 'write a proposal' or 'outline a campaign' or 'write a speech' or uses some other phrase, you are expected to write in **continuous prose**.

  Consequently, the general format – introduction, body, conclusion – is still expected.

  Use the general guidelines for writing essays given at the beginning of this chapter to guide your writing for this module as well.
- Analysis and interpretation are key – read the question carefully.
- Underline key words in the question.

  Examples:

  In an essay discuss how you would organise your campaign.

  Write the proposal you will make to the school administration ...

  Write a speech to the awardees and their parents focusing on respect, tolerance and togetherness.

- Your tone is not just how you say something but also what you say. Choose what you say carefully.

  If you are writing an essay you may need to be more academic, possibly neutral and use technical terms.

  For a speech you are expected to be persuasive. You might use emotive language or humour.
- Your writing should appeal to the audience you are writing for, be it the examiner, the school administration, awardees or parents.

  In an essay, your register should be formal. (An examination is a formal context.)

  In a proposal you are speaking directly to an audience, so too when you are making a speech. Your register, tone and vocabulary should reflect this.
- Create a plan for your response – make notes, in an organised manner, of what you will write and in what order.

Pointers for a campaign

- If you are to do a campaign, you will want to consider how long it will last. (It is more than likely that this will be an extended period of time.)

  Estimate it and state it.
- Remember you will always need to use different strategies with different audiences.

  Use demographics (age, gender, social class, educational background, occupation, etc.) to categorise your target audience if the question does not specify these.

Note

In the exam, many candidates go right into answering this question without writing an introduction and then they end without a conclusion.

This is a costly omission.

Remember that the total marks include marks for organisation, which includes having both an effective introduction and an effective conclusion.

You will lose valuable marks if you omit either of these two elements.

Note that an essay is what is required.

In the essay you are required to explain the manner in which you will plan, structure and conduct the campaign – so you will outline your campaign plan.

Here you have to write a proposal.

You must outline all the ideas, suggestions and approaches you want the school administration to consider. A proposal is a pitch.

In this question you are asked to write a speech directed to two specific audiences on this specific topic.

Remember your register, tone and vocabulary are important in each case and should be varied to suit your audience.

- The words 'media' and 'channel' are sometimes used interchangeably; sometimes the term 'media/channels' is used.

    Part of analysing the question might be to determine what is actually required.

    It could be that both are wanted.

  - Media are **what** you are going to use.

      For example, quizzes, speeches, lectures, text messages, emails, dramatic presentations (skits, dub poems, etc.), advertisements, flyers, songs or jingles, documentaries, etc.

  - Channels are **how** you are going to reach your audience.

      For example, radio, TV, newspapers, PA systems, billboards, noticeboards, the Internet (specify which aspect of this, e.g. social media, and be even more specific if applicable, e.g. YouTube – and say what exactly you will place there), neighbourhood or youth club meetings (as determined by your target audience), school assembly, etc.

Pointers for a speech

Introduction

- Begin with a hook – an opening that catches the audience's attention.
    This should relate to the topic of the speech.
- Give the audience a reason to listen to you – outline why what you are going to say is important to them.
    (Do this without saying 'You should listen to me because …' or 'What I am about to say is important to you because …')
- Outline what you will talk about – this is very much like your thesis statement.
    Remember the topic outlined by the question.

Body

- The body of your speech develops the talking points you mention in your introduction – that is, the things you say you will talk about.
- Use different techniques – rhetorical questions, emotive language, pathos, logos, ethos, humour, anecdotes, using personal pronouns. (Remember you are talking to your audience.)
- Develop each talking point in a separate paragraph.
- Begin each paragraph with a statement that captures the talking point.

    For example, if your speech is about technology in the life of the audience and one of your talking points is that technology controls our lives you may choose to begin a paragraph on this with 'Secondly, my young friends, technology is like an unrestrained pit bull, it's chasing us'.

    This means that in this paragraph you will demonstrate in what way technology is like a pit bull and then how it is chasing us. Importantly, however, you will talk about what this means in relation to technology controlling their lives and yours. Remember that your talking point in this paragraph is that technology controls our lives.

- End each paragraph with a statement that sums up your talking point and positions you for the next one (if that paragraph isn't the last one; if it was, just close).

    For example: 'And that's how the dog chases us … technology … it pushes us, prods us and tempts us to do all manner of evil to keep up with it or outsmart it or prove we are just as smart. Technology threatens to take over our very existence, that is not to say, young folk, that it doesn't have its uses.'

The first part sums up the talking point and the last part – 'that is not to say, young folk, that it doesn't have its uses' – clues the audience in to what is to come in the next.

Conclusion
- End on a high note.
- Reiterate your talking points.
- Challenge your audience – give them a charge or a call to action.
- End with a statement that will have them talking long after your speech is done – it may be a saying, an anecdote, a joke (only if you can pull this off) or an alarming statistic – something that captures the topic of your speech and gives the audience something additional to think about and take away.

Tackling a Module 3 question

Let's look at a specific example of the sort of question you might get on Module 3 in Paper 2.

Read the following scenario carefully then answer the question that follows.

You are a final-year Media and Communications major at your local university and you were selected as class representative. The level of enrolment has dropped over the past five years. You have been asked to speak to a group of final year students from your alma mater who are about to make their selection for university. You want them not only to choose your university but also your programme of study.

a. In no more than 90 words, explain how you would use TWO verbal and TWO non-verbal elements to influence your audience's decision.

b. Prepare the presentation you will make to the students.

c. Discuss how digital technology may aid your presentation.

Total 25 marks

First, analyse the scenario.
Who are you?
- A final-year university student
- A Media and Communications major
- A class representative

What is the situation?
- Enrolment dropped
- Need students to apply
- Students from your alma mater will be choosing universities

What is required of you?
- Get students to choose your university
- Get students to select your programme

Next, determine the format your answer should take.
This is not one seamless essay. There are three distinct parts.

Then, underline key words in the question.

You are expected to write about a paragraph.

What you need to do – outline and justify.

The manner or way.

What you need to talk about and how many.

a. In no more than 90 words, explain how you would use TWO verbal and TWO non-verbal elements to influence your audience's decision.

The purpose for using the elements.

- For this question you need to know how to use different verbal elements (such as language strategies and use of different registers) and non-verbal elements (such as body language, pitch and timing).
- Even though this question requires just a paragraph, treat it as a mini essay.
  It needs:
  - an introduction – i.e. a topic sentence;
  - a body of developmental and supporting sentences;
  - a conclusion – i.e. a summary sentence or statement.
- Use linking words and phrases to make transitions.
  For example, 'The first verbal element …'; 'In addition to the use of anecdotes, another verbal element that I would utilise is a casual register …'; 'The first non-verbal element …'; 'Having discussed the use of anecdotes and a casual register as well as body language and artefacts as the verbal and non-verbal elements, respectively, it is clear that …'

Note that you are not given a word limit, however, you are expected to write an extended piece, similar to an essay.

What you need to do – write out the information you will give to the audience.

The specific audience – who you are presenting to.

b. Prepare the presentation you will make to the students.

- Think about what format this will take – it is not an essay, it is more like a speech.
  Keep in mind the organisational structure.
- Consider the situation you are in and your audience in determining your tone, register and vocabulary.
  - The audience is a group of teenagers and young adults.
  - They are from your alma mater – think about what you have in common.
  - The situation is a presentation so should be relatively formal, however, the audience is young and also from your alma mater so you have a connection with them. Also the aim is to appeal to the audience so you should modify your register accordingly.

What you need to do – talk about it and explain

How it will help

c. Discuss how digital technology may aid your presentation

In what way

What you have to discuss – identify it

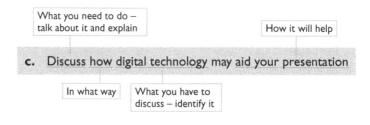

- Identify the digital technology that you would use.
  For example: a virtual tour, a slide show (say of what), video clips (again, say of what).
- Say how you would use each named item.
- Explain how will it help the presentation – you must always give a justification for each choice you make.

Worked example

Read the following scenario carefully then answer the question that follows.

You are a final-year Media and Communications major at your local university and you were selected as class representative. The level of enrolment has dropped over the past five years. You have been asked to speak to a group of final year students from your alma mater who are about to make their selection for university. You want them not only to choose your university but also your programme of study.

a. In no more than 90 words, explain how you would use TWO verbal and TWO non-verbal elements to influence your audience's decision.

b. Prepare the presentation you will make to the students.

c. Discuss how digital technology may aid your presentation.

Total 25 marks

This is the student's introduction. It is simple and it works as it clues the examiner in to what is going to be discussed.

Note that many students present their responses to the Module 3 question using the labels (a), (b) and (c). All responses should be in essay format – including those to the Module 3 question. Essays require an introduction, a body and a conclusion.

The student goes on to explain how the non-verbal elements will influence the audience in the next couple of sentences. What is lacking, however, is an idea of how exactly space and body language will be utilised. Although you are constricted by a word limit, you need to be as clear and detailed as possible.

Since the preceding part of the question asked you for the verbal elements you would use to influence your audience's decision, it is expected that you incorporate the verbal elements you discussed when you write the speech.

Young people are easily distracted and so in addressing them, the communication tools – both verbal and non-verbal – along with appropriate technology needs careful thought in order to maintain their interest. To influence this audience I would use a combination of rhetorical strategies such as ethos and pathos along with a casual register as two verbal elements. These I would pair with proxemics and kinesics as the non-verbal elements. The aim is to have students think seriously about the information presented to them and thus simplify their decision making process. Rhetorical devices will be used throughout the presentation to have students actively thinking about the faculty. Additionally, a casual register will enable me to develop a kinship with the audience and to be more relatable. In this way they are more likely to listen to what I have to say and make a positive decision. By utilising space and body language, I will be able to display my enthusiasm for the programme, thus engaging the audience to develop a interest in the university. These non-verbal elements will also allow me to exhibit to the students the type of characters (e.g. good, friendly and respectful) they would expect to see at the university. These verbal and non-verbal elements will greatly enhance the following speech as outlined to be delivered to this particular audience.

Fellow Fortis brothers, no matter where we go we are 'Fortis forever and forever Fortis'. I am E-Jon Thomas from the University of the West Indies and a final-year student, specialising in the field of Media and Communication. I am here on behalf of the school and my class to promote

---

Here the student has identified the elements that he will be using.

The opening phrase – 'In an effort to influence such an audience ...' – works as a nice link to the introductory sentence.

The student gives a general reason for using the combined elements.

The question requires you to say how the elements will be used and here the student provides such an explanation of how the verbal elements are used.

This is the student's concluding sentence. It has a dual purpose as it concludes the paragraph and also the answer to part (a), and also provides a link to the subsequent paragraph, which is the first paragraph of the presentation and therefore the answer to part (b), by highlighting what is to come.

This first line serves the purpose of building a common bond with the audience.

This paragraph, although in the body of the general essay, serves as an introduction to the speech that the student is presenting.

Note that the student has included relevant information taken from the question and used that as a basis for his introduction.

Note also that his tone is conversational yet formal.

As mentioned in the previous section, you are expected to use an appropriate register and tone for the context given in the question.

the programme. I, like you, was a student of this noble institution. I wasn't sure I would find another school that mirrored the Fortis spirit. In fact, I wasn't sure what I would even want to do if I found such a school. Whilst completing my final year here, I was yet to be sure of my field of choice and some of you may be experiencing the same uncertainty. Today I am here to help you out of that fuzzy zone by pointing you to the one faculty you need to be a part of.

The faculty you choose will be dependent on what you want to do with your life. Right now, you might not have a preferred career but are just looking for a field that promotes innovation and creativity, a field that pays well and allows you to have fun in the process. Well, in that case, Media and Communication is a great field to choose. It gives you great flexibility and allows you to have fun, actual fun, on the job. With a degree in this field one can become a public relations specialist, photographer, reporter, writer or editor, with a salary in the range of 30 to 60 thousand US dollars per annum. The accredited undergraduate programme to get you on this route only takes three years to complete with a manageable tuition of USD$ 3000.

The topic sentence tells the examiner what the paragraph is about and at the same time maintains the link with the preceding paragraph.

I am aware that this tuition fee is hefty to some and therefore if you leave your email address, links will be provided to you to access websites divulging scholarship programmes and their application forms. I, myself, am a beneficiary of a scholarship. In addition to the scholarships available here, there exist international programmes, for those who wish to study for some time overseas. Providing that a minimum GPA of 3.0 is maintained, students can apply to these programmes in their second year.

Note the use of transitions. Remember they help to create a cohesive unit.

If you focus on this PowerPoint presentation, you will see the breakdown of the total tuition you will pay for the programme alongside the minimum potential salary you can make and you will also see how quickly you can recover the money you would have spent. Joining this faculty is an investment in yourself, in your future. Pamphlets are also available to provide you with additional information on scholarship and grant programmes; details on the jobs associated with the field and a lot of other relevant information about my faculty and the field in general. Like any other field, hard work is necessary. Striving for success without hard work is like trying to harvest what you haven't planted. If you join my faculty I guarantee that at the end of the field work you'll find the harvest to be well worth it.

This is the end of the speech. Remember you want to end on a high note that will remain with your audience.

There isn't much of a conclusion but the culminating sentences here do give a sense of completion to the speech.

This topic sentence is simple yet effective.

The preceding speech can only be effective if it is aided by various elements – technology being one. With the use of digital technology, such as microphones, PowerPoint presentations and smart phones or tablets, a presentation can become more interesting or appealing. Such devices help the presenter to appeal to the audio and visual senses thus helping them to conceptualise information. Microphones help in making the presenter audible, and people will focus more on what is being said if

For questions like this you will definitely need to name the technological devices. You do not, however, want it to appear as though these are included without purpose.

they are not straining to listen, which can cause them to lose interest. Although some people learn better through listening, others prefer to see. By using PowerPoint presentations and smartphones or tablets, students will be able to see and not just hear what is being presented to them. Teenagers are strongly attached to their phones so by sending the relevant information, pictures and videos while presenting, some students will be more engaged as they are actively participating in what is going on.

Note the student develops his paragraph by explaining how the devices will aid the presentation.

To sum up, when making a presentation, you must take the audience into consideration and ensure that your speech holds their interest. This means that the verbal and non-verbal elements as presented in preceding paragraphs need to be appropriate for the audience and the message you have to deliver. Added to that, using suitable digital technology can aid your presentation by making it more interesting and engaging.

Note the transitional phrase used to introduce the concluding paragraph.

The student has written an effective conclusion. Note that he has reiterated his points without sounding repetitive and all aspects of the question have been included.

Contributed by E-Jon Thomas, Kingston College

Exercise

Although there were no word limits given for parts (b) and (c), you do have to be able to finish within the time allowed.

This student wrote nearly 1000 words. In addition, part (a) had a word limit of 90 words and the student's response to that part is over twice that length.

Could you write this amount in 50 minutes? How could you revise it to make it more succinct?

Gathering and Processing Information

1. **Read the extract below carefully then answer the questions that follow.**

The most famous walk of all time

'That's one small step for man, one giant leap for mankind.' Astronaut Neil Armstrong started the first walk on the Moon with these famous words. Armstrong and Buzz Aldrin went on the most famous walk in history during NASA's Apollo 11 mission in 1969. We learn about the first Moon landing in school, but we rarely hear many details about what that walk was actually like and what they saw during this incredible moment in history. This wasn't just the first walk on the Moon; it was the first walk on another world. These men are two out of only 12 human beings to have stepped off a spaceship and on to 'alien' soil. The Moon was host to a walk that was truly out of this world.

The view they experienced as they stepped out of the lunar module was like nothing they had seen before. The perception of distance didn't work the same way as on Earth. Looking to the horizon, things that were far away, looked very near. The Moon was playing tricks on their eyes. The short radius of the Moon made its curvature visible from where they stood. Despite taking their walk in the morning, the sky was jet black. Unlike the star-filled skies of the Earth, on the Moon, every star's light was blocked by the intensely sunlit ground of the Moon. Only the bright, blue and white Earth interrupted the darkness. It was a brilliant jewel that hovered over 238,000 miles away.

The area of the Moon where their trailblazing walk occurred, called the Sea of Tranquillity, is not really a sea at all. It is a 4-billion-year-old desert. It is covered with moon dust, like the rest of the Moon's surface. Armstrong told Aldrin, 'It has a stark beauty all its own, like the high desert of the United States.' Aldrin, however, called the view 'magnificent desolation,' finding it fairly menacing. Looking at the ground as they began their walk, Armstrong became fascinated by the moon dust's behaviour. Made of silicon dioxide glass created by meteoroid strikes on the Moon's surface, and other minerals, the moon dust didn't act like dirt on a dusty trail, rising up in clouds all around. When kicked, Armstrong said the moon dust rose and formed a shape like a flower petal frozen in the vacuum of space.

A walk on the Moon means feeling as light as a feather. Neil Armstrong described it as a 'very pleasant kind of place to work in,' because things weighed less on the Moon due to its weaker gravity. Because of the force of gravity being only about 17% of what it is on Earth, as well as wearing cumbersome spacesuits that were developed for protection rather than movement, the astronauts couldn't just walk along as they would at home. When the astronauts tried walking like we do here on Earth, they flew up into the air and fell over. So, the walking style that they developed was more like a 'hopping run' than a walk. The Moon became a giant trampoline, encouraging the astronauts to jump higher as they went.

Everyone, throughout history, will remember this amazing walk. Although it was a lonely walk on a new world for the two astronauts to take, millions of people all over the world were with them every step of the way as they watched live on TV. It has captured the imagination of people for decades, inspiring children everywhere to look up at the Moon's friendly face and imagine a place where they too might one day take the walk of a lifetime.

References:
Npr.org, 'Neil Armstrong talks about the first moon walk', December 8, 2010, Robert Krulwich

Soil Science Society of America. 'NASA's Dirty Secret: Moon Dust' *Science Daily*, 29 September 2008

Nasa.gov

a. In not more than 30 words, state the writer's main point.

b. Write an ESSAY of not more than 500 words in which you

    i. state the writer's purpose;

    ii. discuss strategies and language techniques used;

    iii. evaluate the reliability of the information presented.

Total 25 marks

Module 2 Practice question for Paper 2

Language and Community

2. Read the poem below carefully then answer the question that follows.

Hurricane Bangarang

Dem say lightnin no strike twice ina di same place
    An mi granny always say 'no dash waata ina God face'
    So all when mi bex say mi spend up hol heep a money pan hurricane
tingz
5   Mi teng Gad Matthew stap brabs in im tracks wid him rains an wid
him winds.
    But what wi would a do ee, if this storm did really drop
    Fi come tear dung wi tree dem an tek off wi roof top.
    A no all a wi lucky so, caz some a wi neighbours get a beatn
10   Matthew carry on bad, without rhyme an widout reason.
    I never could understand though how hurricane know when dem
season start
    Or choose dem landin spot or decide which paat dem ago walk.
    Do they have a board meeting? Itemize a scheduled plan?
15   Do they have a blue print flying around with in dem destructive hand?
    How dem see so good out a dem one yeye, fi tek on so much force
    An why dem always come ina night like dem is some kinda ghost?
    No! A serious question dem, mi really haffi aks….
    So, you are telling mi dem question de never cross yu thoughts?
20   As me look bak pahn weda history, not to be a chauvinistic lad
    Compare to oman hurricane, di man dem no too bad.
    Dem kaaz far less damage to di place dem we dem choose fi lan.
    If yu tink a lie mi lie, compare Katrina an Sandy to Gilbert or Ivan.
    Dem say hurricanes originate a Africa, so maybe that is why
25   Is vengeance for all the tears wa dem foremothers cry
    I don't mean to start a revolution or cause an argument to this effect
    Jus a share mi thoughts out loud so you really don't haffi bex.
    Let me leave this hurricane argument alone yaa, an just give thanks
likkle more

30   Caz di next hurricane is Nicole, an wi no want she fi ketch to category four.

Extract from 'Hurricane Bangarang' by Charity Barrett © 2016

In an ESSAY of no more than 500 words, discuss

a. the appropriateness of the writer's choice of language;

b. three linguistic characteristics that would make it difficult for a non-Creole speaker to understand the poem;

c. how communication could be enhanced through a video presentation of this poem.

Total 25 marks

Module 3 Practice question for Paper 2

Speaking and Writing

3. Read the following scenario carefully then answer the question that follows.

You are a member of your school's 'Technological Innovators Club'. You and your fellow club members have designed an app that assesses and measures student productivity. Although the app is very useful, it potentially infringes on students' privacy. Your club members want to test the app on your school population. Your principal has agreed to give your group a hearing where you will present a proposal on how you plan to conduct this test. Afterwards he and his team will consider whether to grant permission for the test run.

In ESSAY format, write the PROPOSAL that you will present to the principal and other administrators for consideration. Your proposal should include details of:

a. the application, including its name and potential problems;

b. your plan for persuading students and parents to participate in the test run;

c. the language varieties and registers you consider appropriate for engaging the two audiences named in part (b);

d. two media/channels to be used to launch the application and present the idea to the student population and their parents.

Total 25 marks

Chapter 6

Preparing a portfolio

Objectives

By the end of this chapter you should be able to do these things:

- speak and write with effective control of grammar, vocabulary, mechanics and conventions of speech and writing in the use of Caribbean Standard English;
- present information in speech and writing with accuracy, clarity and fluency;
- demonstrate competence in organising oral and written communication;
- gather information about current issues;
- evaluate information about current issues and present it in an appropriately structured oral and written form;
- create a portfolio of oral and written work.

Tips

- Always refer to the syllabus for the word count for each section. It is important to respect the word counts. You will not gain marks by going over.
- Also check in the syllabus the number of marks awarded to each section.
- Proofread your portfolio for Standard English grammar, punctuation and spelling before your final submission. If you are not good at proof-reading your own work, consider peer review and have one of your classmates or a friend proofread it for you.
- Any sources you use in creating your portfolio, must be properly documented and credited in a bibliography. Not doing this will be taken as an indication of your attempt to plagiarise – pass off someone else's ideas or work as your own. This is a criminal offence.

Introduction

The portfolio – or Internal Assessment (IA) – represents 20% of your CAPE Communication Studies final exam grade. The aim is to test your level of competence in utilising the knowledge and skills you should have acquired through your exposure to the three modules. It provides you with an opportunity for self study and to put into practice many of the theoretical concepts involved in Communication Studies.

The portfolio covers the following:
- Expression both oral and written
- Comprehension
- Critical skills
- Summary skills
- Evaluating sources
- Organising skills

You will be required to choose a theme on which the components of your portfolio will be based. Your chosen theme must relate to your academic choices, future career path and personal interests.

You will need to draw on everything you have learned during the course as the portfolio captures objectives from all three modules, although much of it may be focused on Module 1.

How to structure your portfolio

Your portfolio must be divided into four sections:
1. General introduction
2. Exposition (orally presented speech)
3. Reflection (preface and creative piece)
4. Analysis

Each section is looked at in more detail later in this chapter.

Make sure you also include a bibliography citing all your sources, and a conclusion.

Choosing your theme

To begin preparing for your portfolio you will need to decide on a theme. Your entire portfolio will be based on this theme.

- Choose a topic or current event that you are passionate about and can research by interviewing experts, collating and analysing data.

   The more knowledgeable about the theme you are, the better your portfolio and exposition will be.

   Therefore choose a theme that interests you and that you either want to find out more about or that you want to share your knowledge and enthusiasm about.

- Choose a theme that has some connection to the three main aspects of your life – personal, academic and work-related.

- Choose a theme that will allow you not only the opportunity to collect data during research but also one that will lend itself to creative development – that is, one that will allow you to write a creative piece informed by data collected during your research.

   Remember that this needs to be a creative literary piece and not a news report or essay.

- Do not simply use themes that were used by your friends in previous years or that you researched for Caribbean Studies.

   Think of things that have an impact on you at home and school, among friends, things you hear on the news or see happening daily – things that have captured your interest.

   Ask yourself:
   - Are any of these connected to my academic life?
   - Are any of these connected to my personal life?
   - Do any of these tie in with my career aspirations?

   You want to settle on an idea that, when you create a spider diagram with it written in the centre, has clear connections with the three areas of your life as per the syllabus requirements.

- Be sure to choose a theme for which you can get local and/or regional data.

- Before making your final decision, ask these questions:
   - Is there a local organisation or ministry or individual who can assist with data and interviews?
   - What can I learn and share that will be of interest and will provide enough material from which to create a reflective piece?
   - What communication devices will I be using in my creative piece?

Suggested themes

These are just a few ideas. They are by no means comprehensive and you need to be sure that the theme you choose is of interest and relevance to you.

- Athletics in the Caribbean
- Social media and the teenage identity
- The influence of the media on Caribbean language development
- Death and the teenage psyche
- Skin bleaching
- Dancehall culture and young men

- Abortion – the male perspective
- Contemporary lifestyles and morality
- Violence at school
- Discipline in schools: a precursor to discipline in society
- Accessibility of tertiary education
- The impact of pop culture on the idea of beauty in the Caribbean
- New millennium jobs

Researching your theme

Once you have selected your theme, you are ready to begin your research.

You will need to complete your research, or at least the majority of it, before you begin to draft any of the sections of your portfolio because you need to know enough about your theme to write a good exposition and reflection.

Research can be conducted using:

- personal interviews;
- the Internet;
- local resources, such as local organisations, government agencies, local media;
- books and journals.

Although much of your research will not appear in your final portfolio, it will show in the depth of your oral presentation and help to inform your writing of the reflection.

As you learnt in Module 1 – Gathering and Processing Information – you will need to focus on the essential information and ensure that it supports or highlights the theme you have selected.

Make a list of questions based on your idea.

Think about:

- Who?
- What?
- Where?
- Why?
- How?

For example, if your portfolio is on teenage pregnancy, you may start your research with these questions:

- Who is defined as a teenage mother?
- What organisations and/or government agencies works with teenage mothers?
- Where do teenage mothers seek advice?
- Why is teenage pregnancy seen as an issue within our society?
- How can teenage mothers be assisted?

There are more details on researching a theme later in this chapter, in the section on the exposition.

> **Tip**
>
> The more you read about and understand your topic, the better your portfolio and, in particular, your presentation will be.

The general introduction

The general introduction is that part of your IA that gives a synopsis of your portfolio.

It is worth 12 marks and should not exceed 200 words.

There are three specific things that need to be mentioned in this introduction and marks are allocated for each of these.

1. **Identify the theme and purpose**
   - This accounts for 2 of the 12 marks.
   - State clearly your theme and topic.
   - There should be no question or confusion after the examiners have read your statement outlining these two things.
   - Then explain your purpose – give your reason(s) for delving into the topic, what motivated your choice and what you hope to achieve from researching this topic. Ultimately your purpose should explain your end goal.

2. **Explain how the theme is treated in the exposition and reflection sections**
   - This accounts for 4 of the 12 marks.
   - Remember that your IA has an oral component and a written component.
   - You need to explain what aspects of the theme you discussed in the exposition. That is, tell the examiners what information about your theme you discussed in your exposition.
   - You also need to say how the exposition helps you to achieve your purpose.
   - Then you need to explain how the theme is treated in the reflection section. That is, outline how you brought out the theme in the creative piece that you have written.
   - You also need to say how the creative piece helps you to achieve your purpose.

3. **Explain how the theme relates to your academic, work-related and personal interests**
   - This accounts for 6 of the 12 marks, divided equally between the three aspects.
     This means that if you fail to provide information on any one of the aspects you will lose a third of the marks.
   - The three areas are academic, work-related and personal interests.
   - You need to explain clearly the connection between your theme and each of the three areas. You can treat them in any order.
     - Say how some aspect of your personal life has motivated your choice of theme or how researching the theme will be of use in your personal life.
     - Say how the theme is related to you in your prospective field of work – what the relationship is between the theme you are researching and the career path you want to pursue.
     - Say how the theme is related to your current studies – what in your experience as a student has prompted you to select this theme.

Tip

It is generally best to write the general introduction last, since then you will have completed all the relevant sections that need to inform your writing of this component.

You can structure your general introduction into three paragraphs that cover the areas that you are to deal with.

Remember that in order for you to maximise your grades you must fully and clearly deal with each requirement.

Example: General introduction

The purpose in researching the theme is clearly stated.

The treatment of the theme in the exposition is clearly stated.

The student tells the examiners what the exposition deals with and how this is done in a way that helps the researcher to achieve the purpose outlined in the first paragraph.

She states the relation to her academic interests.

She states the relation to her career aspirations.

'Emotional abuse' is an issue that is often downplayed. This research therefore focuses on its effects on young adults in the Caribbean in an effort to highlight the severity of the issue with the hope that it will be taken more seriously.

The theme was highlighted in the exposition, which presented research findings about the damaging and long-term effects that emotional abuse has on young people. Additionally, a narrative entitled 'Blue Rage', tells the story of a woman and her family trapped in a cycle of emotional abuse and the resulting behavioural and mental problems displayed by her and her children. The story is a real-life example of the psychological effects of emotional abuse and how it is manifested.

This topic became of interest to the researcher through a discussion of a character's mental health issues brought out in a novel being studied for CAPE Literature. As a future social worker and psychotherapist interested in working with troubled youths, this theme will help the researcher better recognise symptoms displayed by the emotionally victimised. On a personal note, the researcher has a relative who is emotionally abusive to his child and hopes that the findings of this research can be used in helping both of them.

This student outlines her theme and topic. Note that there is a clear distinction between the two and the topic has two variables – effects of emotional abuse and young adults in the Caribbean.

The treatment of the theme in the reflection is clearly stated.

The student identifies the genre of the reflective piece, gives the title of the piece and briefly states what it is about.

In the last sentence she shows how the piece contributes to the purpose.

She states the relation to her personal interests.

The exposition

Mark allocation

There are 16 marks in total for the exposition.

Discussion of issues – 5 marks

Evaluation of information – 4 marks

Organisation – 3 marks

Delivery – 4 marks

This is the mark allocation at time of writing. Check your syllabus to ensure there have been no changes.

The exposition is the oral component of your portfolio.

It is worth a total of 16 marks.

It requires that you plan, prepare and practise a speech that you present to be examined.

The speech must have the same theme as the rest of your portfolio.

You will have ten minutes in which to present.

Note that this is not an expository essay. Rather it is a discussion that presents:

- the issues raised – your research findings;
- the challenges experienced while conducting your research;
- how valid and reliable the information you gathered is, taking into account the effect of source, context and medium/channel.

Your exposition must be well organised.

It should have an introduction, a body in which your ideas are developed and a conclusion.

The organisation of your exposition accounts for 3 of the 16 marks.

Bear in mind that you are allowed one cue card measuring 4 by 6 inches.

It can have relevant headings only, no additional information and will be checked by your teacher before you begin.

What does the syllabus really require?

A discussion of the issues raised

This means that you are to talk, in detail, about the information that you uncovered during your research.

It should include varying points of view and opposing positions relating to your topic.

This must be done with examples and evidence.

For example, if your topic is 'The phenomenon of world-stage police brutality and the spill-over effects on the Caribbean', some possible issues being raised during your research could include the view that 'police brutality in foreign countries is too far removed to have any real impact on the Caribbean' or that 'the Caribbean has had its own issues with police brutality and so what is happening on the world stage is inconsequential' or that 'more economically developed countries set a precedent for the rest of the world and so the prevalence and rise in police brutality evident in the Caribbean today is a direct by-product of what is happening on the world stage'.

A discussion of the challenges experienced in exploring your topic

This means that you must outline some of the problems you faced and had to overcome while researching and collecting data on your theme.

The problems may be physical or non-physical.

For example, a physical challenge might have been constant disruption from outside elements during an interview and a non-physical challenge might have been a difficulty finding data relevant to the Caribbean situation.

These two requirements, a discussion of the issues raised and of the challenges experienced together account for 5 of the 16 marks available.

An evaluation of the information gathered

Here you are being asked to make a value judgement.

You need to determine whether the information you have gathered is accurate and true and whether it can be accepted as being sound, rational and incontestable.

You do this by presenting an evaluation of the sources, contexts and mediums/channels you used to obtain data and whether they satisfy the criteria for being reliable and valid.

This evaluation accounts for 4 of the 16 marks available.

Planning and preparing for the exposition

Select your theme and topic

If you have not already done so, this is obviously your first step.

Do not forget that your theme and topic are distinct.

To help with the distinction, think general and specific, respectively.

The theme is general, a broad concept or idea, and the topic focuses on a specific aspect in relation to that theme.

Example:

Theme: The use of drugs in sport

Topic: The impact of doping on athletics in Jamaica

Remember that your topic needs to be current and researchable.

To ensure that your topic is researchable ask yourself these questions:

- Does my topic have more than one variable, or element?
- Consider the topic in the example: the variables include the impact of doping and athletics in Jamaica. (You may even consider athletics and Jamaica as separate variables.)
- Is there a question within the topic that requires an answer?
- The question can be directly stated or implied.
- Will I be able to collect data to answer the question related to my topic?

So, essentially your topic should be a question with at least two variables, which allows for data collection that leads to answers to the question. It should not, therefore, have a moral or ethical premise.

Identify data sources and evaluate them

- You will need to draw on Module 1 content as you will need to use your knowledge about evaluating sources to guide you.
- Review the section on evaluating information in Chapter 2.
- Remember that in the exposition you will need to present an evaluation of your sources.
- Once you start your preliminary research and identify some primary and secondary sources, you will want to determine if they may prove useful to you.
- With regard to books and articles (physical or electronic), the author, publication date and information about where and by whom it was published are necessary in order to assess the usefulness of the source for your research.
  - Try to find information that will tell you about the author's credentials, institutional affiliation, experience, area of expertise and other related published works.
  - The date of publication should also be taken into consideration as you need data that is up-to-date.
  - Looking at who published a book or where an article was published will also help you determine the reliability and validity of your data.
- You need to ensure that the sources you have selected are relevant, valid and credible.
- Make note of these sources and the details that you verified in your evaluation. You will need this for the exposition.

Collect data

This will ensure that all your information is in one place and it will be easier to access and review.

- You now need to utilise appropriate data collection tools to gather your information.
- You need to collect at least two pieces of related data on the selected topic.
- This means that you will need to find data from no fewer than two sources.

Exam Tip

Have a notebook specifically for the expository section.

Put all your notes, jottings and summaries in it.

- Examine the content.
  You want to ensure that the information is relevant to your topic and does not contain author biases.

  The sources you select should also have content that can be verified and should either support other materials or provide new information – this may even be an opposing viewpoint.

  Scan the content and make notes as you go along.
- Once you are satisfied that the content is useful and fulfils the criteria for being valid and reliable, summarise the data and be sure to identify your sources.

  Note that these must be referenced in the bibliography. Do **not** plagiarise.

  Make a note whether the sources are primary or secondary.

  You should aim, where possible, to have at least one of each.
- Note that even when you have used questionnaires or interviews to collect data from primary sources, you still need to review the data and summarise it.
- This is the information you are putting together for that part of your exposition that requires a discussion of the issues. Remember your variables and find suitable literature that allows you to provide definitions for each of them.
- Make a note of all the challenges (physical or otherwise) you encounter as you go through the research process.

Plan your speech

Remember that the exposition is an oral presentation and that it should take not more than 10 minutes.

There are two possible approaches to planning your speech.

You can either write your speech in its entirety or you can create an outline for it.

Your teacher may well require that you write out your speech.

Whether you write the entire speech or just an outline, you must ensure your speech:

- has the appropriate structure, that is, an introduction, a body and a conclusion;
- covers all the required areas.

Use the mark scheme in your syllabus when reviewing your speech to ensure that you have all the requisite parts.

Below is a suggested outline. Naturally you can modify it according to personal style or the requirements of your teacher.

Introduction

Suggested time: 2 minutes.

- Begin with an interesting opening – something that will capture the attention of the examiner.

  This may be a quote, a proverb, a line from a song, a joke, etc.

  Ensure that whatever you use is relevant to your theme and what you will be presenting.
- State the topic.
- Define the variables.
- Discuss the background to and/or the historical development of the issues.
- Make mention of differing views on the topic.

- State your interest In the topic (your reasons and motivations for investigating the topic).
- Give your thesis statement.

Body paragraph 1

Suggested time: 2½ minutes.

- Discuss the issues.
  - Identify each source by name and point of view on the issue.
  - Give a summary of the information gathered from your sources.
  - Present information that both agrees and disagrees with your thesis statement.
- Discuss the challenges you experienced in exploring the topic. You need to show that you have an understanding of the impact of these challenges on the research process and/or the data collected.

Body paragraph 2

Suggested time: 2 minutes.

- Evaluate the effect of Source 1.
  - Explain how the source was useful in providing information on the topic.
  - Explain why you believe the **source** is qualified to give relevant information on the issue, or not.
  - Explain specifically why you believe **information** from this source is believable and reliable, or not.
  - Say how you believe the **context** within which the source operated might have affected the information it gives.
  - Explain how the **medium/channel** by which the information was conveyed has affected the credibility of the message.

Body paragraph 3

Suggested time: 2 minutes.

- Evaluate the effect of Source 2 in the same way as above.

Conclusion

- Suggested time: 1½ minutes.
- Give a brief summary of your main points.
- Give a brief statement of how you have benefited from the research process.
- Make a final judgement as to whether the information you collected is valid, credible and reliable.
- Make recommendations where necessary.

Practising your speech

- Practise your speech in front of the mirror.
- Present to family and friends and ask them for feedback.
- Record yourself and review it so you know what aspects of the speech and your delivery you need to work on.

Presenting your exposition

- You need to speak for a maximum of 10 minutes with only one 4 by 6 inch cue card as a prompt.
- The delivery of your speech accounts for 4 of the 16 marks available.
- The examiner will determine your marks based on your audibility, fluency, eye contact, body language and paralinguistic features such as timing and pitch.
- To maximise your marks, you need to plan your speech and practise it. It is important that you know your presentation. This does not mean that you should write it out and learn it word for word. It means that you should be so familiar with the content that you are able to confidently convey your ideas.

- Do not rush or speak too quickly. You should already know how long each section of your speech will take.
- Your presentation should be done confidently and show a thorough interest and understanding of the topic chosen – beyond the title of your presentation.
- Keep your voice clear and audible at all times.
- Remember that your body language should enhance your presentation, not detract from it.
- Refrain from clearing your throat and using interjections such as 'hmm', 'like' and 'er'.
- Exhibit good paralinguistic control – use relevant pauses; raise or lower your voice as need be for effect.
- Maintain eye contact and remain calm and self-assured throughout to help convey confidence.
- If you miss something or make a mistake, continue (pause briefly if you need to but try not to lose composure) and do not allow yourself to be thrown off.
- Remain pleasant throughout your presentation and end by thanking the examiner for listening.

The reflection

The reflection section of your portfolio is worth 14 marks.

The creative piece is worth 10 of the 14 marks available for this section.

The marks are awarded for:

- creativity – this includes use of the genre and audience engagement as well as originality;
- organisation – as with all writing, the presence of a beginning, a middle and an end and good linkage between them and with the theme;
- expression – this includes appropriateness of register, grammar, punctuation, vocabulary and also careful proofreading.

You are required to write an original creative piece in a literary genre of your choice – a drama (a play or monologue), a poem, a short story or diary entries.

There is a word limit of 800 words and the piece must relate to your theme and help to achieve your purpose.

- Bear in mind that your creative piece should contain the features of that genre.

  For example, if you are writing a play, it must contain the characters' names with their dialogue beside it, together with stage directions and other features of a play.
- Remember that the piece **must** contain **two** linguistic elements that you can analyse in the next section of your portfolio.

To accompany the creative piece, you must write a preface.

This has a word limit of 200 words and is worth 4 of the 14 marks allocated to the reflection.

Tip

Although the preface precedes the reflection in the portfolio, it is a good idea to write it after you have written your creative piece. This will ensure that the preface accurately reflects the content of your writing and that it makes sense.

Tip

A lot of students state that they are writing for a general audience.

Try not to let that be your choice.

The preface

The preface is an introduction to the reflective piece. In it you should explain:

- the purpose of the piece;
- the intended audience;
- the context for presenting the piece.

You can present the three aspects in three paragraphs.

1. The purpose

- Introduce your theme and give some background information about the issues.
- You may also want to identify the genre and title of the piece.
- Explain the purpose for which the piece was written.

2. The intended audience

- Explain who you are writing for – who you want to read the piece that you have written.
- Explain why you want to reach this particular audience. This should relate to achieving the purpose you have outlined in the preceding paragraph.

You need to be specific – you are writing for policy-makers in the government or the parents of preteens or young athletes in high schools, for example.

3. The context

- The mistake that many students tend to make is to explain the context as the setting of their creative piece. This is **not** the context that is being referred to.
- In this paragraph you need to explain to the examiner where you would publish the piece so that the intended audience have access to it.

  For example, a magazine, an anthology, a newspaper, via a specific social media platform, on a noticeboard, etc.
- Once you have identified the context, be sure to say why this context is effective.
- Always remember to connect everything you say to your purpose. Naturally your reason for selecting a particular context must be how effective it is in reaching your target audience.

Example: Preface

Note that here the student tells the reader the theme as well as the topic.

Lottery scamming is an escalating criminal activity which instigates violent crimes, especially in tourist destinations. The purpose, therefore, of this one-act play is to show the connection between lottery scamming and violent crimes and ultimately increase awareness of the issue and reveal other aspects of the country that are being negatively impacted.

The student outlines the purpose of the reflection.

She states the intended audience.

The intended audience includes members of law enforcement and law-abiding citizens. Law enforcers are responsible for organising initiatives to seek out and remove criminal elements from society and law-abiding citizens have a responsibility to assist with this mission. Many citizens feel that since they are not being scammed, they are not affected by what is happening but it is a national concern.

She gives a clear explanation of her choice of audience.

The student gives specific details about the context.

The play will be recorded and published via YouTube with links posted on Facebook, and also be sent as an email attachment to police personnel via the JCF intranet. YouTube is one of the most frequently accessed video-sharing platforms, and with links posted to Facebook the video is more likely to go viral, thus reaching the target audiences identified. Additionally, the JCF intranet is used specifically for communicating with law enforcement and therefore this target group will have direct access to the message.

The student explains her choice of context.

Writing your reflection

- Remember that the reflection is a creative literary piece. It must be an original piece written by you, based on your theme and topic and must include linguistic features that you can analyse.
- First, choose the genre.
- Ask yourself:
  - What do I enjoy reading or listening to?
  - Which genre will best suit my creative project?
  - What am I good at writing?
  - Can this genre accommodate the four linguistic features (registers, dialectal variation, attitudes to language and communicative behaviours) that need to be included?
- Next, brainstorm ideas and make notes.
    Remember that this piece must be based on your theme and, even though you are not writing a news report, the theme must be reflected throughout.
- Create an outline.
    Whatever genre you decide to use, there must be a beginning, a middle and an end.
- Pen your first draft. There will be many drafts before you get to a finished product. Do not destroy any previous draft. You may need to review them for ideas or inspiration or just for notes so you can improve a subsequent draft.
    Be sure to include all four linguistic features.
- Even though you will only be discussing two in your analysis, the reflection needs to have all four and must have sufficient examples of each.
    Write with these features in mind.
    Revise as you go along.
- Each genre has specific characteristics.
    Review them and write the piece so that stylistically it stays true to the form you have selected.

Notes

- Do **not** use obscene language in your work and refrain from including graphic accounts of sexual activity.

  These will not earn you extra marks, quite the opposite.

- Remember the piece **must** be your own work.

  You cannot use someone else's work nor can you include any part of someone else's work in your own work.

  If you do this you are plagiarising, which is a serious offence for which you will be penalised.

  Your work will be checked for plagiarism.

  In addition, you cannot submit a creative piece that you have previously submitted for a grade, to CXC® for instance. This too is considered plagiarism (self-plagiarism) and you may be similarly penalised.

For example, if you are writing a short story, be sure to use the appropriate format for the dialogue. Similarly if you are writing a play, you do the same. A play has certain conventions that are very different from a story, and a poem has conventions that are different again.

- Write clearly and concisely. Your creative piece, irrespective of genre, must tell a story, and that story must relate to your theme.
- Present a draft to your teacher and then edit subsequent drafts as instructed or needed.

Tip

If you are discussing dialectal variation, it would be best not to discuss registers as your second feature.

The problem is that the two are very close and you do not want to limit yourself or repeat the examples.

Be sure to review the various definitions before you begin to write so you are clear in your mind how and why each is used and you can identify suitable examples to support your discussion.

You can only use examples from your creative piece.

Tip

Remember the N-I-E principle – **n**ame, **i**llustrate, **e**xplain.

The analysis

In this section you are required to present an analysis of your creative piece.

You are expected to select any two of these four linguistic features:

- registers
- dialectal variation
- attitudes to language
- communicative behaviours

and analyse their use in the piece.

This means you need to have included them in your creative piece.

- **Do** name the features you will discuss.
- Do **not** give a definition of the features.
- **Do** illustrate their use by providing examples of the two features being discussed.
- **Do** give a full explanation of why the feature was used and how they conveyed the theme.
- Do **not** analyse all four features.

For this analysis you are given a 350-word limit and are expected to follow the appropriate essay-writing structure. That is, there should be an introduction, a body with appropriate and relevant transitions and a conclusion.

The analysis is worth 18 marks.

- 8 of the marks are awarded for the content.
- 5 of the marks are awarded for expression.
- 5 of the marks are awarded for organisation.

Structure of the analysis

You can present your analysis as four paragraphs.

Introduction
- Give a synopsis of the creative piece.
    This is likely to include the genre, title, point of view and what the piece is about.
- Remember that your analysis should say how the theme is reflected in your writing.
    Consequently, in the introduction be sure to introduce your theme by stating how it is reflected in your creative piece.
- For example:
    Throughout the play, it can be seen clearly how warped and evil the antagonists have become and the terror they cause in the lives of people through mass killings, arson and rape simply because of their involvement in lottery scamming.

- The last sentence in your introduction should indicate the two linguistic features that you will discuss.

Body paragraph 1: Linguistic feature 1
- Identify the linguistic feature that you will discuss in this paragraph. This must be the feature that was named first in the introduction.
- Say which characters use the feature or different aspects of the feature, give examples and then explain why they are used.
- For example:

> Both casual and consultative registers are used in the piece. The casual register is used mostly between Maka Don and JP. One example is when JP enters the scene and Maka Don says, 'Yes daag, si di real shella come een ya now' and JP's response was 'Mmmhmm, so we di man dem a deal wid?'. The familiarity with which they speak indicates that they are close friends, which justifies the use of this register. The consultative register is used between Don Man Dread and JP. This is illustrated when Don Man Dread says, 'So tell me again why the drop late' and JP replies, 'w-w-wi couldn't find di location, Sir.' Don Man Dread's tone and language clearly indicate that he is the one in charge and he uses that register to emphasise his position. JP's register here is very different from the informal way he conversed with Maka Don and is due to the formal relationship with his boss.

Body paragraph 2: Linguistic feature 2
- Identify the linguistic feature that you will discuss in this paragraph. This must be the second feature identified in the introduction.
- Handle the discussion in the same way that you handled the discussion of the first feature.
  - Name – identify the feature and the characters who use it.
  - Illustrate – give examples.
  - Explain why the choices were made.

Conclusion
This does not need to be long – two or three sentences.

You simply need to reiterate how the creative piece conveyed the theme and features you discussed.

Final notes

The internal assessment is your opportunity for self study and it is possible to earn full marks on your portfolio. You simply need to follow the relevant guidelines and the mark scheme as outlined in the syllabus and create for yourself an excellent portfolio.
- Ensure that you complete all four sections and cover all the requirements of each.
- Review your portfolio for errors and omissions. Proofread as many times as you need to.
- Start preparing right away. Plan ahead or plan to fail. You need to use your time wisely to prepare the best portfolio.
- Do not forget to include a suitable conclusion to your project. In this you should reflect on the process of writing and share your opinions and insights.
- You must include a bibliography to credit your sources. Review and use an appropriate format for writing a bibliography.

Audioscripts

Chapter 1 Extract

This track is available at https://www.collins.co.uk/page/Caribbean.

A House for Mr Biswas

It had been a year of scarcity, of rising prices and fights in shops for hoarded flour. But at Christmas the pavements were crowded with overdressed shoppers from the country, the streets choked with slow but strident traffic. The stores had only clumsy local toys of wood, but the signs were bright as always with rosy-cheeked Santa Clauses, prancing reindeer, holly and berries and snow-capped letters. Never were destitutes more deserving, and Mr Biswas worked harder than ever. But everything – shops, signs, crowds, noise, busyness – generated the urgent gaiety that belonged to the season. The year was ending well.

By V.S. Naipaul

Chapter 2 Extract 1

This track is available at https://www.collins.co.uk/page/Caribbean.

Squatters' Rites

Peas, corn, potatoes; he had
planted himself
king of a drowsy hill; no one
cared how he came to such green dignity,
scratching his majesty
among the placid chickens

But after a time after
his deposition, the uncivil wind
snarled anarchy through that
small kingdom. Trees, wild birds
troubled the window,
as though to replace the fowl
that wandered and died of summer;
spiders locked the door,
threading the shuddered moths,
and stabbed their twilight needles through
that grey republic. The parliament of dreams
dissolved. The shadows tilted
where leaf-white, senatorial lizards
inhabited his chair.

By Dennis Scott

Chapter 2 Extract 2

This track is available at https://www.collins.co.uk/page/Caribbean.

The Virgins

Down the dead streets of sun-stoned Frederiksted,
the first free port to die of tourism,
strolling at funeral pace, I am reminded
of life not lost to the American dream;
but my small-islander's simplicities
can't better our new empire's civilized
exchange of cameras, watches, perfumes, brandies
for the good life, so cheaply underpriced
that only the crime rate is on the rise
in streets blighted with sun, stone arches
and plazas blown dry by the hysteria
of rumour. A condominium drowns
in vacancy; its bargains are dusted,
but only a jeweled housefly drones
over the bargains. The roulettes spin
rustily to the wind; the vigorous trade
that every morning would begin afresh
by revving up green water round the pierhead
heading for where the banks of silver thresh.

By Derek Walcott

Answers

Chapter 1
Listening comprehension

1. B
2. B
3. C
4. C
5. B
6. D
7. A

Chapter 2

1. B
2. D
3. C
4. B
5. D
6. B
7. A
8. A
9. B
10. B
11. D
12. C
13. A
14. D
15. D
16. C
17. B
18. A
19. B
20. C
21. D
22. B
23. A

Chapter 3

1. C
2. A
3. D
4. D
5. B
6. C
7. D
8. C
9. B
10. B
11. C
12. C
13. D
14. C
15. A

Chapter 4

1. D
2. D
3. C
4. B
5. D
6. B
7. C
8. D
9. B
10. A
11. D
12. C
13. B
14. D
15. A

Index

NOTES

Acknowledgements

The authors and publishers would like to thank the following students for providing sample answers for the worked examples:

Shamar Wedderburn, Kingston College (Module 1 essay, pages 121–2)

Sadé Rodney, a graduate of St Andrew Technical High School (Module 2 essay, pages 126–8)

E-Jon Thomas, Kingston College (Module 3 essay, pages 133–5)

Photo credits: Chapter 1: George Rudy/Shutterstock; Chapter 2: Monkey Business Images/ Shutterstock; Chapter 3: Goran Bogicevic /Shutterstock, Inc.; Chapter 4: William Perugini/ Shutterstock; Chapter 5: William Perugini/Shutterstock; Chapter 6: Daniel M Ernst/Shutterstock

NOTES